The Scientification of Love

Revised Edition

MICHEL ODENT

'an association in which the free development of each
is the condition of the free development of all'

FREE ASSOCIATION BOOKS / LONDON / NEW YORK

First published 1999 by
Free Association Books Limited
57 Warren Street, London W1T 5NR

www.fa-b.com

Reprinted with revisions 2001

ISBN 1 85343 476 0 hbk

A CIP record for this book is available from the British Library.

10 09 08 07 06 05 04 03 02 01

10   9   8   7   6   5   4   3

Designed, typeset and produced for Free Association Books by
Chase Publishing Services, Fortescue, Sidmouth, EX10 9QG
Printed and bound by CPI Group (UK) Ltd, Croydon, CR0 4YY

THE SCIENTIFICATION OF LOVE

Until recently Love was the realm of poets, artists and philosophers. In the closing decades of the twentieth century, it has been studied from a variety of scientific perspectives. It is easy to miss the importance of the phenomenon because there is a multitude of specialised approaches to exploring the nature of Love. Authentic scientific advances always lead to new questions. This is the case of the 'Scientification of Love', which suggests simple and paradoxically new questions, such as:

- How does the capacity to love develop? Today all scientific data converge to give a great importance to early experiences, particularly to a short critical period immediately after birth.

- What are the links between the many facets of Love? We suddenly think of raising the question that way because biological sciences suggest an answer.

- Why all societies ritually disturb the first contact between mother and baby, for example by transmitting the belief that colostrum is tainted or harmful? One must keep in mind that during a long phase of the history of mankind there has been an evolutionary advantage in developing the human potential for aggression rather than the capacity to love. During many millennia the basic strategy for survival of most human groups has been to dominate Nature and to dominate other human groups.

At a time when humanity must invent radically new strategies for survival, the 'Scientification of Love' is presented as the most vital aspect of the scientific revolution and as a landmark in the history of humankind.

For several decades Michel Odent has played multiple and complementary roles in influencing the history of childbirth and health research. As a practitioner he developed the maternity unit at Pithiviers Hospital (France) in the 1960s and 1970s. He is familiarly known as the obstetrician who introduced the concepts of birthing pools and home-like birthing rooms. His approach has been featured in eminent medical journals such as the *Lancet*, and in TV documentaries such as the BBC film *Birth Reborn*. After his hospital career he specialised in home birth practices.

As a researcher he founded the Primal Health Research Centre in London, whose objective is to study the long-term consequences of early experiences. An overview of the Primal Health Research data bank (available on the net at www.birthworks.org) clearly indicates that our health is shaped during the primal period (from conception until the first birthday). It also suggests that the way we are born has long-term consequences in terms of our sociability, our aggressiveness or, in other words, our capacity to love.

Michel Odent developed a preconceptional programme (the 'accordion method') in order to minimise the effects of intra-uterine and milk pollution by synthetic fat soluble chemicals such as dioxins, PCBs, etc. He is currently conducting research into the non-specific long-term effects on health of early multiple vaccinations.

He is the author of about 50 scientific papers and 10 books published in 20 languages. In his books he developed the art of reversing traditional questions: how to develop good health, instead of how to prevent diseases, or how the capacity to love develops, instead of how to prevent violence.

Contents

Foreword

Miriam Stoppard

It is more than twenty years since I arrived in Pithiviers with a film crew to take a look at the work of Michel Odent, a French surgeon who was gaining notoriety as a revolutionary obstetrician.

Even then he did not fit into any tidy medical slot. He had been trained as a surgeon and, bringing his objectivity and common sense to obstetrics, was confounded by what he found: outdated practices defying logic and science but nonetheless accepted for years without question and which, by their very nature, prolonged labour, worsened pain, increased the risk of a complicated delivery and therefore the chance of medical interventions.

Through the simple expedient of allowing women to respond to their birthing instincts, to give birth in soft rather than high-tech surroundings, to be joined by partners who would help and (literally) support them, he turned obstetric practice on its head and reduced medical interventions, such as forceps delivery and caesarean section, virtually to nil.

I found it an irresistible thesis. I can remember doing a spontaneous ad-libed 'outro' to my TV documentary on the steps of his hospital where I gave vent to my feelings of outrage that I had been cheated of Odent's kind of birth. That I had given birth to two babies according to the inflexible, hierarchical system then in fashion in the UK, on my back, legs in stirrups, pushing the baby out uphill! It was only through talking to Odent that I realised that women, if they stood upright, could harness the force of gravity to *pull* the baby out.

His approach was sane, humane and based on freeing the animal instincts of women who are giving birth. But the clincher for me was that he demystified and demedicalised the process of birth for women, babies and men.

Eager that all women should benefit from his rethinking of childbirth, I immediately set about incorporating his theories and practices into my books. Indeed, his teachings became the lynchpin of my writing on pregnancy and birth and I have included a passage about them in every book I have written on the subject since.

Women and doctors alike owe a great debt to Odent. We need visionaries like him. It strikes me that his latest hypothesis, contained in this book, is visionary too. He holds out the rather surprising promise that a study of how we learn to love, starting at the breast a few seconds after birth, may hold a clue to the cause of violence in our society.

He suggests that love (or attraction) has its roots at cellular level, on the surface of cells in fact, in the form of receptors, which bind to (or bond with) 'informational substances' – ligands – chemicals with messages attached. This phenomenon of locking on can be seen as love at a molecular level and, as you would expect, it is highly selective. Just as each caterpillar has its own particular leaf, each ligand has only one receptor which it can lock on to, or love.

The hypothesis comes together in the study of oxytocin, the hormone of labour, childbirth, lactation and yes, you've guessed it, mother-love. Indeed, almost any kind of love: women and men release oxytocin during sexual activity too.

He may be right again, as he was last time with birth, that this capacity to love – encapsulated in the not very complex molecule of oxytocin – and especially the capacity to love and protect our planet, is the prerequisite of global survival.

Acknowledgements

I must acknowledge my indebtedness to all the mothers (and grandmothers) who helped me to conceive this book and who participated in its development. In particular:

Susan Colson – from our fruitful conversations new concepts emerged, such as 'the scientification of love' or the 'scientification of breastfeeding'. I admire your ability to replace inappropriate terms by 'le mot juste'.

Moyra Bremner – thank you for teaching me everything about the suffix '-ation'.

Jane Feinmann – thank you for helping me to re-write a key chapter.

Alice Charlwood – thank you for your precious advice.

Elisabeth Geisel – thank you for giving me a translation of the most important chapters of your acclaimed book. Now I understand the role of tears in the expression of emotions.

Liliana Lammers – thank you for your holistic understanding of the word 'Love'.

Preface

It is a bit risky to write an inter-disciplinary book in an age of over-specialisation. I anticipate that some readers – who are experts in their own field – will regard parts of this book as superficial or simplistic. I also anticipate that some chapters may occasionally seem difficult or cumbersome, with a lot of irrelevant or useless details.

In spite of such difficulties this book is necessary at a time when people are focusing on violence and the roots of violence. I am convinced that we can go a step further in our understanding of the many aspects of violence by turning the question on its head and looking instead at how the capacity to love develops. I will never forget that I had a new vision of the fight against disease on the day I started to investigate the roots of good health.

In an attempt to cope with the difficulties of a book destined to have a very diverse readership, I have added a summary at the end of each chapter, together with a list of references for those who wish to study more thoroughly some particular aspects of a new, yet immense, topic.

To Eugene Marais,
whose mirror was not broken

Introduction – The Power of Love

Every human being can experience love, yet it remains difficult to define, much less experiment on. It lies at the heart of poetry, art, philosophy, religion and much popular culture; but love has hardly been seen as a suitable subject for scientific study.

When Teilhard de Chardin predicted, fifty years ago, that humans would one day learn how to harness the energies of love and that such a development would be as pivotal in the history of mankind as the discovery of fire, his vision was regarded as purely utopian. Not so today, for in the closing decades of the twentieth century the nature of love and how the capacity to love develops has become a subject for scientific study, the implications of which are at least as important as those of genetics, electronics or the quantum theory. Yet this work is far from the realms of popular science and most scientists, including the medical profession, are hardly even aware of this new area of knowledge.

The main reason for this widespread ignorance is that scientific research has become highly specialised. The new scientific data about love in all its manifestations is emerging from a multitude of disciplines. Experts who have detected small yet vital details in the jigsaw of this new area of research are unaware of or are unable to see the way their findings link up with other pieces of research. I also happen to believe that some topics of research have been regarded as politically incorrect and have been deliberately neglected. Again and again I have come across important studies that have been ignored despite their resonance and significance.

This book is an attempt to change all that. The scientification of love has vital lessons for the general public as well as professional medics or scientists. Firstly, it demonstrates that, of all the different manifestations of love – maternal, paternal, filial, sexual, romantic, platonic, spiritual, brotherly love, not to mention love of country, love of inanimate objects, and compassion and concern for Mother Earth – the prototype of all these ways of loving is maternal love. What is more, the evidence points to a short and yet critical period of time just after birth which has long-term consequences so far as our future capacity to love is concerned. We disregard the consequences of ritualising, interfering with or otherwise neglecting the physiology of that critical period at our peril.

Secondly, science now reveals that the various ways that we love are actually wholistic in the sense that the same hormones are involved, and the same patterns of behaviour occur during sexual intercourse, childbirth and breastfeeding. Understanding that concept helps us to realise the price the human race has paid for 'civilisation', culminating in the current widespread problems of low sex drive, difficult childbirth and difficulties in breastfeeding. It also points the way to how we can achieve a better experience of our sexuality.

Above all, the scientification of love can engender a new awareness, and perhaps a radical reconsideration of what we want from civilisation. Almost every successful civilised culture shares the same basic strategy for survival, which is to dominate nature and exercise power and control over other human groups. If these cultures have survived to the present day it is because they have successfully developed the human potential for aggression. At the beginning of the twenty-first century, developing the capacity to love and respect each other, as well as Mother Earth, is at long last becoming a prerequisite for global as well as individual survival.

That is why Teilhard de Chardin's 50-year-old prediction must become a reality.

1   Prehistory – The Unbroken Mirror

The scientification of love has had a prehistory, and it requires a great deal of patience and luck to detect prehistoric events. It was by chance that I became aware of the work of Eugene Marais who was known to a whole generation of Afrikaans-speaking South Africans as a poet who wrote about pain and love. He should be more well known for his scientifically minded hypotheses and his studies of animal behaviour which came long before other, more widely acclaimed, mainstream research.

Around 1920 – prehistoric times as far as this subject is concerned – Marais was making experiments to confirm his intuition as a poet that a connection exists between the pain of birth and maternal love.[1] He studied a group of sixty Kaffir Bucks, knowing that there had not been a single instance of a buck mother in the herd rejecting her young in the previous fifteen years. He proceeded to give the birthing females a few puffs of chloroform and ether, and noticed that the mothers refused to accept their newborn lambs afterwards. Of course, at that time Marais was not in a position to interpret the nature of the links between pain in childbirth and maternal behaviour. He did not know about hormones and he did not have the means to explain how the natural painkillers released in labour by the birthing mother also play a role in inducing maternal behaviour. However, he had established a simple rule by comparing the behaviour of different species – when newborns are immature and reliant upon a loving and nurturing mother, there is a correlation with painful birthing. If Marais' reports had been originally published in English and so more well known, certain theories about pain in human childbirth being 'cultural' would never have been proposed or widely accepted – or perhaps they would have been formulated in more subtle ways. In the middle of this century it was common to claim that childbirth should not be painful because there is no other example of a physiological function which is painful in the normal course of health, or to claim that pain in childbirth is 'reflexoconditional'.

The experiment by Eugene Marais gives us a first opportunity to evaluate the relevance of animal experiments in improving our knowledge of human nature. It indicates the limits of what we can learn from this approach.

The conclusions of animal experiments are often simple and unambiguous: the buck mothers did not take care of their babies. We know why the behaviour of human beings is much more complex. Human beings communicate with language. They create cultures. Their behaviour is less directly influenced by their hormonal balance. When a woman knows that she is expecting a baby, she can anticipate displaying some maternal behaviour. This does not mean that we cannot learn from non-human mammals. Animal experiments indicate the questions we should raise about ourselves.

Where human beings are concerned, the questions must include the word 'civilisation'. If mother bucks do not take care of their babies after giving birth with a few puffs of ether and chloroform, this suggests that we should be wondering about the future of our civilisation if the birth process is routinely disturbed in that way.

The experiment by Eugene Marais also gives us an opportunity to clarify how we use science to improve our understanding of life in general, and of human nature in particular. The biological sciences represent a sort of mirror in which we can look for a reflection of ourselves.

When the scientification of love was in its 'prehistoric' phase the mirror was not very well polished. The image was fuzzy, details indistinct. But it was still possible to see the whole of the unpolished mirror in its entirety. Eugene Marais could study life and human nature from an impressive number of perspectives. A poet, who had studied religion, law and medicine, he was also a journalist and a practising advocate, and he spent a great deal of his time analysing the behaviour of animals as varied as termites, scorpions and baboons. His capacity to establish constant links between so many perspectives was at the root of his deep understanding of love, pain and human nature.

Today the same mirror is brilliantly polished. Infinitely small details may be detected, but it is as though the mirror is broken in thousands of pieces. Experts who know so much about a tiny piece of the fragmented mirror are unable to see the way it links with the other pieces that make up the whole.

Our task is to rebuild a picture on as large a scale as possible. We do not underestimate the difficulties. We will start by establishing links between the largest pieces brought to light by scientists of different disciplines. Then we will look at many small pieces that are still difficult to relate to each other.

Summary

The metaphor of the mirror is central to our description of the phenomenon we call the 'scientification of love'. The biological sciences represent a mirror in which we look for a reflection of ourselves. Today that mirror is brilliantly polished, but it is broken into thousands of pieces. Our objective is to establish links between all these tiny pieces.

Reference

1 Marais, E.N. *The soul of the white ant*, with a biographical note by his son. Methuen, London, 1937.

2   Learning from Ducklings,
        Sheep and Monkeys

The actual history of the scientification of love started in the 1930s with an experiment which has become a legend. The founder of modern ethology, Konrad Lorenz, reported that one day he had interposed himself between newly hatched ducklings and their mother and then imitated the mother duck's quacking sounds. These ducklings became attached to Lorenz for the rest of their lives, following him when he walked in the garden, for example. This is how the concept of a sensitive period in the process of forming attachment was introduced, and it shows that there is a short yet crucial period immediately after a birth which will never be repeated.

Ethologists observe the behaviours of animals and human beings. They are not interested in any particular animal; they often study one particular type of behaviour in a number of unrelated animals.[1] Although they try to interfere as little as possible, they make experiments. This is how many of them came to study the process of attachment between mother and child. They all confirmed that in a great variety of species of birds and mammals there is a sensitive period just after birth.

For example Bridges studied in particular the birth of rats.[2] If a mother rat is disturbed when giving birth, not only will the delivery be delayed but also there will be long-term effects on the young through an altered mother–young relationship. The long-term effects can also be detected when mothers are either permitted or not permitted to lick their young at birth. Those which lick them can have them removed and, 25 days later, they are more responsive to pups than those which have not licked them. Furthermore, Bridges evaluated the amount of contact with maternal behaviour: if pups were left with newly delivered mothers for 4 to 6 hours after birth, the mothers would behave maternally, even after a 25-day separation. Siegel and Greenwald also studied the loss of maternal behaviour after early separation between mother and babies among hamsters.[3]

The consequences of mother–infant separation at birth are still more spectacular among sheep and goats than among rodents, since maternal responsiveness wanes more rapidly among these species. Another difference from the rodents is that ewes and dams develop individualised bonds to their young and butt away any alien young animals. Among these herd animals with syncronised reproduction the risks of exchanges are high. As early as 1956 Blauvelt demonstrated that if a baby goat is separated from its mother for only a few hours before the mother has a chance to lick it, and the kid is then given back to her, the mother 'seems to have no behavioural resources to do anything further for the newborn'.[4] Among sheep, Poindron and Le Neindre found that if separation between mother and lamb begins at birth and lasts for 4 hours, half the ewes would not take care of their lambs afterwards.[5] In contrast, if a 24-hour separation begins 2 to 4 days after the birth, all the ewes would accept their lambs again afterwards. It is also among ewes that Krehbiel and Poindron verified the link between the birth process and maternal behaviour. When ewes have given birth with epidural anaesthesia they do not take care of their lambs.[6]

The studies by Harlow have many practical implications.[7] First, he studied the interaction between mother and baby primates – a species closely related to humans. Also, as a scientist, he did not hesitate to use the word 'love' when he explored links between two different aspects of it, manifested in the mother–baby relationship on the one hand, and in adult sexual behaviour on the other hand. The use of the word 'love' by ethologists such as Harlow gives a first opportunity to underline the way in which scientific studies of love run into major difficulties. The main problem is that the meaning of the word cannot be explained or defined because love has so many facets. However, there are obvious links and similarities between the different expressions of love and it seems that the ethologists, including Harlow, have come to a tacit agreement that the attachment between mother and baby is the prototypical form.

Harlow took newborn monkeys away from their real mothers between six and twelve hours after birth. He gave them instead two artificial mothers; one made of wire and the other made of cloth. The wire-mesh dummies were fitted with a bottle to feed the babies, but the babies rarely stayed with the wire dummies longer than it took to get the necessary food. They clearly preferred cuddling with the softer cloth dummies, especially if they were scared. Baby monkeys without real mothers became socially in- competent. They engaged in stereotyped behaviour patterns such as clutching themselves and rocking constantly back and forth; they exhibited excessive and misdirected aggression. When older they were often unsuccessful at mating. Frequently, when a surro- gate-raised female was approached by a normal male, she would sit unmoved, squatting upon the floor. In contrast, a surrogate- raised male might approach an in-oestrus female in a strange way, for example clasping the head instead of the hind legs. However, females who became mothers tended to be indifferent or abusive towards their babies, to the point that many of them died.

We should bear in mind that ethologists can also study human behaviours. The point is that the limits between human ethology and clinical observation are imprecise. However, I want to exclude from our topic observations by practitioners and theories expressed by practitioners. The work of Mary Salter Ainsworth, for example, is undoubtedly in the field of ethology. First in Uganda, and then in the USA, she used authentic ethological methods to study the effects of brief separations of mothers and babies, and the reactions of the babies when they were reunited with their mothers.[8] Certain well-known animal ethologists also studied human behaviour. Eibl-Eibesfeldt, a disciple and colleague of Konrad Lorenz, designed clever methods in order to explore universal behav- ioural patterns. He used a special camera with a lateral lens to study flirting behaviour in a great number of cultures, including industrialised countries.[9] He described flirting patterns and he demonstrated that the gaze is probably the most striking human courtship ploy. When reading about such ethological studies I cannot help thinking about how human mothers are fascinated by the gaze of their newborn babies.

Summary

Ethologists, who observe the behaviours of animals and human beings, regard the attachment between mother and baby as the prototypical form of love. Whatever the species, immediately after birth there is a short yet critical period of time which has long-term consequences.

References

1 Lorenz, K. *Studies in animal and human behaviour*, 2 vols. Cambridge University Press, Cambridge, 1970–71.
2 Bridges, R.S. 'Parturition: its role in the long-term retention of maternal behavior in the rat.' *Physiol. Behav.* 1977; 18: 487–90.
3 Siegel, H.I., Greenwald M.S. 'Effects of mother–litter separation on later maternal responsiveness in the hamster.' *Physiol. Behav.* 1978; 21: 147–9.
4 Blauvelt, H. 'Neonate–mother relationship in goat and Man.' In B. Schaffner ed. *Group processes*. Josiah Macy Jr Foundation, New York, 1956.
5 Poindron, P. and Le Neindre, P. 'Hormonal and behavioural basis for establishing maternal behaviour in sheep.' In Zichella, L. and Panchari, R. eds *Psychoneuroendocrinology in reproduction*. Elsevier–North Holland Medical Press, Amsterdam, 1979.
6 Krehbiel, D. and Poindron, P. et al. 'Peridural anaesthesia disturbs maternal behaviour in primiparous and multiparous parturient ewes.' *Physiology and Behavior*. 1987; 40: 463–72.
7 Harlow, H.F., Harlow, M.K. and Hanson, E.W. In Rheingold, H.R. ed. *Maternal behavior in mammals*. John Wiley, New York, 1963.
8 Ainsworth, M.S. and Bowlby, J. 'An ethological approach to personality development.' *American Psychologist*, 1991; 46: 333–41.
9 Eibl-Eibesfeldt, I. *Human ethology*. Aldine de Gruyter, New York, 1989.

3   Love Hormones and Childbirth

A First Historical Experiment

The scientification of love entered a new phase in 1968 when Terkel and Rosenblatt injected virgin rats with blood taken from mother rats within 48 hours of their giving birth.[1] The virgin rats behaved like mothers. Terkel and Rosenblatt had demonstrated that, immediately after birth, there are hormones that influence maternal behaviour in the blood of mother rats. They repeated their primary experiment with more elaborate techniques, highlighting the importance of the period surrounding birth.

This historical experiment was followed in the 1970s by a great number of other experimental studies exploring the behavioural effects of hormones whose levels are fluctuating in the period surrounding birth. Rosenblatt and Siegel, in the USA, who were studying rats,[2] and Poindron and Le Neindre in France, who were studying sheep,[3] looked in particular at the effects of oestrogens and progesterone. Zarrow and co-workers looked at the effects of prolactin.[4] An overview of all these studies leads us to the conclusion that oestrogens stimulate maternal behaviour and that the rapid decline in levels of progesterone which occurs in the period surrounding birth contributes to the manifestation of maternal behaviour.

A Second Historical Experiment

It is surprising that we had to wait eleven years after the primary experience of Terkel and Rosenblatt before hearing of studies about the behavioural effects of the hormone oxytocin. It is surprising because all physiologists, doctors and midwives know that this hormone – released by the posterior pituitary gland – is essential during the birth process and lactation. It stimulates uterine contractions for the birth of the baby and the delivery of the placenta. It stimulates the 'milk ejection reflex'. It is probably because the peripheral mechanical effects of this hormone were too well known that researchers were not considering its possible behavioural effects. Another reason for such a delay is that oxytocin must be injected directly into the brain to induce detectable behavioural effects. A new era of research started when we learned from Prange and Pedersen that an injection of oxytocin in the cerebral ventricles of mammals can induce a maternal behaviour.[5]

The explosion of research triggered by such an experiment is illustrated by the publication by the New York Academy of Sciences, in 1992, of a 500-page book including 53 articles on the behavioural effects of oxytocin![6] Niles Newton summarised the lesson we can learn from this generation of research by claiming that 'oxytocin is the hormone of Love'. It is noticeable that whatever the facet of Love we consider, oxytocin is involved. It is involved in lactation. During intercourse both partners – female and male – release oxytocin. We can even conclude from the studies by Verbalis that, when we share a meal with other people, we increase our levels of the 'Love hormone'.[7] To share a meal is more than merely to be fed; it is also a way to establish links with your companions. At the very time when the behavioural effects of oxytocin were confirmed by a multitude of studies, K. Uvnas-Moberg, in Sweden, was emphasising that the peak levels of oxytocin just after birth can be still higher than during labour.[8]

Complex Hormonal Balances

There is no contradiction between our current understanding of oxytocin as the hormone of love and the observations of those who studied the effects of other sexual hormones, in particular oestrogens and progesterones in the 1970s. Today it is well understood that oestrogens activate the oxytocin- and prolactin-sensitive receptors. We must always think in terms of hormonal balance. For example, immediately after birth, oxytocin – an altruistic hormone – and prolactin – a mothering hormone – complement each other.

It was also in 1979 that the maternal release of morphine-like hormones during labour and delivery was demonstrated,[9,10] and the release of these endorphins is now well documented. In the early 1980s we learnt that the baby also releases its own endorphins in the birth process and, today, there is no doubt that, for a certain time following birth, both mother and baby are impregnated with opiates.[11,12] The property of opiates to induce states of dependency is well known, so it is easy to anticipate how the beginning of a 'dependency' – an attachment – will be likely to develop.

Even hormones of the adrenaline family (often seen as hormones of aggression) obviously have a role to play in the interaction between mother and baby immediately after birth. During the very last contractions before birth the level of these hormones in the mother peaks. That is why, as soon as the 'foetus ejection reflex' starts, women tend to be upright, full of energy, with a sudden need to grasp something or someone. They often need to drink a glass of water, just as a speaker may do in front of a large audience. One of the effects of such adrenaline release is that the mother is alert when the baby is born.[13,14] Think of mammals in the wild, and we can more clearly understand how advantageous it is for the mother to have enough energy – and aggressiveness – to protect her newborn baby if need be. It is also well known that the baby has its own survival mechanisms during the last strong, expulsive contractions, and releases its own hormones of the adrenaline family.[15] A rush of noradrenalin enables the foetus to adapt to the physiological oxygen deprivation specific to this stage of delivery. The visible effect of this hormonal release is that the baby is alert at birth, with eyes wide open and dilated pupils. Human mothers are fascinated and delighted by the gaze of their newborn babies. It is as if the baby was giving a signal, and it certainly seems that this human eye-to-eye contact is an important feature of the beginning of the mother–baby relationship among humans.

The highly complex role of hormones of the adrenaline–noradrenaline family in the interaction between mother and baby has not been studied for a long time. A small number of animal experiments open the way to further research. Mice who lack a gene responsible for the production of noradrenaline leave their pups scattered, unclean and unfed – except if they are injected with a noradrenaline-producing drug when giving birth.[16]

Our current knowledge about the behavioural effects of different hormones involved in the birth process helps us to interpret the concept of a sensitive period introduced by ethologists. It is clear that all the different hormones released by the mother and by the baby during labour and delivery are not eliminated immediately. It is also clear that all of them have a specific role to play in the later interactions between mother and baby.

Summary

Recently there has been an explosion of studies exploring the behavioural effects of the hormones involved in different episodes of sexual life – intercourse, childbirth and lactation. Today oxytocin appears to be an important 'hormone of love'. By adopting a hormonal approach we can interpret the concept of the critical period which has been introduced by ethologists. The different hormones that are released by the mother and baby during labour and delivery are not eliminated immediately after birth, and they all play a specific role in the interaction between mother and baby.

References

1 Terkel, J. and Rosenblatt, J.S. 'Maternal behavior induced by maternal blood plasma injected into virgin rats.' *J. Comp. Physio. Psychol.* 1968; 65: 479–82.

2 Rosenblatt, J.S., Siegel, H.J. and Mayer, A.D. 'Progress in the study of maternal behavior in the rat: hormonal, nonhormonal sensory and development of aspects.' In Rosenblatt, J.S. et al. ed. *Advances in the study of behavior*, vol.10. Academic Press, New York, 1979.

3 Poindron, P. and Le Neindre, P. 'Hormonal and behavioural basis for establishing maternal behaviour in sheep.' In Zichella, L. and

Panchari, R. eds *Psychoneuroendocrinology in reproduction.* Elsevier–North Holland Medical Press, Amsterdam,1979.

4 Zarrow, M.X., Gandelman, R. and Renenberg, V. 'Prolactin: is it an essential hormone for maternal behavior in the mammal?' *Horm. Behav.* 1971; 2: 343–54.

5 Pedersen, C.A. and Prange, J.R. 'Induction of maternal behavior in virgin rats after intracerebroventricular administration of oxytocin.' *Pro. Natl. Acad. Sci.* USA 1979; 76: 6661–5.

6 Pedersen, C.A. et al. eds 'Oxytocin in maternal, sexual and social behaviors.' *Annals of the New York Academy of Sciences* 1992; 652.

7 Verbalis, J.G., McCann, M., McHale, C.M. and Stricker, E.M. 'Oxytocin secretion in response to cholecystokinin and food: differentiation of nausea from satiety.' *Science* 1986; 232: 1417–19.

8 Nissen, E., Lilja, G., Widstrom, A.M. and Uvnas-Moberg, K. 'Elevation of oxytocin levels early post partum in women.' *Acta Ostet. Gynecol. Scand.* 1995; 74: 530–3.

9 Csontos, K., Rust, M. et al. 'Elevated plasma beta endorphin levels in pregnant women and their neonates.' *Life Sci.* 1979; 25: 835–44.

10 Akil, H., Watson, S.J. et al. 'Beta endorphin immunoreactivity in rat and human blood: Radio-immunoassay, comparative levels and physiological alternatives.' *Life Sci.* 1979; 24: 1659–66.

11 Moss, I.R., Conner, H. et al. 'Human beta endorphin-like immuno-reactivity in the perinatal/neonatal period.' *J. of Ped.* 1982; 101; 3: 443–46.

12 Kimball, C.D., Chang, C.M. et al. 'Immunoreactive endorphin peptides and prolactin in umbilical vein and maternal blood.' *Am. J. Obstet. Gynecol.* 1987; 14: 104–5.

13 Odent, M. 'The fetus ejection reflex.' *Birth* 1987; 14: 104–5.

14 Lederman, R.P., McCann, D.S. et al. 'Endogenous plasma epine-phrine and norepinephrine in last trimester pregnancy and labour.' *Am. J. Obstet. Gynecol.* 1977; 129: 5–8.

15 Lagercrantz, H. and Bistoletti, H. 'Catecholamine release in the newborn infant at birth.' *Pediatric Research* 1977; 11: 889–95.

16 Thomas, S.A. and Palnuter, R.D. 'Impaired maternal behavior in mice lacking norepinephrine and epinephrine.' *Cell.* 1997; 91: 583–92.

4   The Primal Health Research
Perspective

Our research centre – the Primal Health Research Centre – has established a data bank with hundreds of references of studies published in authoritative scientific and medical journals (see www.birthworks.org/primalhealth). All these studies have explored the links between the 'primal period' and health and behaviour later on in life. According to the interpretation I proposed for this term in the past, the 'primal period' includes foetal life, the period surrounding birth and the year following birth.[1]

From an overview of our data bank it appears that when researchers explored the background of people who have expressed some sort of *impaired capacity to love* – either love of oneself or love of others – they always detected risk factors in the period surrounding birth. Furthermore, when such correlations have been highlighted, it was always about an important issue specific to our time. We need to bring together these studies in order to realise how convenient and how new is the concept of impaired capacity to love.

Violent Criminality

Juvenile violent criminality is undoubtedly topical. It can be regarded as a form of an impaired capacity to love others. Adrian Raine and his team, from the University, Los Angeles, California, followed up 4,269 male subjects born in the same hospital in Copenhagen.[2] They found that the main risk factor for being a violent criminal at age 18 was the association of birth complications, *together* with early separation from or rejection by the mother. Early maternal separation-rejection by itself was not a risk factor.

Self-Destructive Behaviours

Teenage suicide, previously almost unknown, is another important issue specific to our time. Lee Salk and colleagues, from
New York, researched the backgrounds of 52 adolescent suicide
victims who died before their 20th birthday, and compared
them with 104 controls.[3] They found that one of the main risk
factors for committing suicide during adolescence was resuscitation at birth. Bertil Jacobson, from Sweden, studied in particular
how people commit suicide. In his first study he looked at birth
record data gathered for 412 forensic cases comprising suicide
victims and compared these with 2,901 controls.[4] He found that
suicides involving asphyxiation were closely associated with
asphyxiation at birth; suicides by violent mechanical means
were associated with mechanical birth trauma. In his last study,
Jacobson confirmed that men (but not women) who had
traumatic births are five times more at risk of committing
suicide by violent means than others.[5] Jacobson explored the
background of 242 adults who committed suicide by using a
firearm, or by jumping from a height, or by jumping in front of a
train, or by hanging, or by laceration, etc. He compared them
with 403 siblings born during the same period and at the same
group of hospitals. Many possible confounding factors were
considered. The differences between men and women disappeared if their mothers had used pain killers of the opiate family
when in labour. It seems that the long-term side effects of pain
killers such as morphine or different sorts of synthetic morphine are different. They include drug addiction.
    Jacobson also studied *drug addiction*. He and Karin Nyberg
looked at the background of 200 opiate addicts born in
Stockholm from 1945 to 1966 and took non-addicted siblings
as controls.[6] They found that if a mother had been given certain
pain killers during labour, her child was statistically at increased
risk of becoming drug-addicted in adolescence. More recently,
Karin Nyberg and colleagues confirmed such results among
American subjects.[7] They found that three doses of opiates or
barbiturates given to the mother at birth were associated with a
five-fold increase in the risk of the child becoming addicted.

Anorexia nervosa is also a form of self-destructive behaviour. The only study of anorexia nervosa included in our data bank detected correlations with the birth itself.[8] A team of researchers had access to the birth records of all girls born in Sweden from 1973 to 1984. They also had access to the files of 781 girls aged between 10 and 21 who had been admitted to a Swedish hospital for the treatment of anorexia nervosa. For each anorexic girl, five non-anorexics born in the same hospital during the same year were selected for comparison. It appeared from this authoritative study that the most significant risk factor for anorexia nervosa is a cephalhaematoma at birth, that is a bloody collection between two layers of one of the skull bones. A cephalhaematoma indicates that the birth was highly traumatic from a mechanical point of view. A forceps delivery or a ventouse were also risk factors.

Autism and other aspects of the 'autistic spectrum' can also be presented as the expression of an impaired capacity to love. Autistic children and autistic adults do not socialise. When teenagers they cannot manage dating. When adults they do not have children. My interest in autism started in 1982, when I met Niko Tinbergen, one of the founders of ethology, who shared the Nobel prize with Konrad Lorenz and Karl Von Frisch in 1973. As an ethologist familiar with the observation of animal behaviour, he studied in particular the non-verbal behaviour of autistic children. As a 'field ethologist' he studied the children in their home environment. Not only could he offer detailed descriptions of his observations, but at the same time he listed factors which predispose to autism or which can exaggerate the symptoms.[9]

He found such factors evident in the period surrounding birth: 'deep forceps' delivery, birth under anaesthesia, resuscitation at birth and induction of labour. When I met him he was exploring possible links between difficulty in establishing eye-to-eye contact and the absence of eye-to-eye contact between mother and baby at birth. His data were not presented in statistical language and he had no control groups. However the work of Tinbergen (and his wife) represents the first attempt to explore autism from a 'primal health research' perspective.

It is probably because I met Niko Tinbergen that I read with special attention, in June 1991, a report by Ryoko Hattori, a psychiatrist from Kumamoto, Japan.[10] Mrs Hattori evaluated the risks of becoming autistic according to the place of birth. She found that children born in a certain hospital were significantly more at risk of becoming autistic. In that particular hospital the routine was to induce labour a week before the expected date of delivery and to use a complex mixture of sedatives, anaesthesia agents and analgesics during labour.

Interest in such studies is enhanced at a time when we know more about the hormonal profile of autistic children and the particularities of their brain structures. Oxytocin, in particular, appears to be a promising avenue of research. Let us recall once more that oxytocin – which is instrumental in contracting the uterus for the birth of the baby and the delivery of the placenta – is also an altruistic hormone, a 'hormone of love'. It seems that the oxytocin levels are comparatively low in autistic children, and there have been attempts to treat some of them with oxytocin. I assume that one day the way autistic children release oxytocin will be explored. It seems that oxytocin is more effective when released rhythmically, in a succession of fast pulsations. Today it is not impossible to measure the rhythmicity – the pulsatility – of oxytocin release.

The results of the main studies which have detected links between how people are born and different forms of an impaired capacity to love have been published in very authoritative medical journals. However they are comparatively unknown and are not taken into account in most subsequent articles. This is a common characteristic between them. For example a large review article in the *British Medical Journal* about autism did not mention any of these studies exploring correlations with the primal period. One might also wonder why most of these studies were not repeated by a greater number of researchers.

Can Research be Politically Incorrect?

Because I have personally met the authors of all these studies, I can offer some pertinent comments about this family of research. Before he died of a stroke Niko Tinbergen sent me a series of letters. He was surprised that a majority of child psychiatrists 'find his methods, facts and views difficult to accept'. He added that he felt 'rather suspect and rejected by the profession'. During one of my trips to Japan I met Ryoko Hattori. After she published her data about autistic children in 1991 she was made redundant as a psychiatrist at the university hospital. Because of that she was forced to abandon any hope of enlarging or repeating her studies. I once had a conversation with Lee Salk, who studied teenage suicide from a primal health research perspective. He was disheartened and surprised by the lack of response to his findings. Soon after, he died of cancer. Bertil Jacobson, who studied all sorts of self-destructive behaviour had difficulty overcoming major obstacles created by ethical committees which prevented him from accessing birth records so he too was unable to further his studies. The thesis of Karin Nyberg about 'studies of perinatal events as potential risk factors for adult drug abuse' was originally refused at Karolinska Institute, without any technical, ethical or scientific reason – an unprecedented scandal. As for Adrian Raine, who is originally British, he faced dozens of refusals of his research projects in the United Kingdom before finding an opportunity to achieve his goals in Los Angeles.

Can research be politically incorrect?

I recently coined the term 'cul-de-sac epidemiology' when referring to studies that are not replicated, even by the original investigator.[11] This framework includes research about topical issues (juvenile criminality, teenager suicide, drug addiction, anorexia nervosa and autism are good examples). Despite the publication in authoritative medical or scientific journals, the findings are shunned by the medical community and the media. I used this term to contrast with the term 'circular epidemiology' which has been used in order to describe a tendency to constantly repeat the same studies, even when there is no doubt about the results.

Starting from foetal life

All the previous studies were retrospective. This means that researchers looked at children, teenagers or adults who had something in common (they were murderers, drug addicts, etc.) and explored their background. There are also, in our data bank, prospective enquiries and in particular studies whose objectives were to evaluate the possible long-term effects on the offspring of the emotional state of the mother when she was pregnant. Several of these studies suggest that the emotional states of the pregnant women may have long-term effects in the fields of sociability, aggressiveness or – to put it another way – the capacity to love.

The oldest of these studies comes from Finland. Two psychologists identified 167 children whose fathers had died before they were born. They also indentified 168 children whose fathers had died during the children's first year of life.[12] Then they followed all 335 of these children through 35 years of medical records. All the children grew up fatherless. Only those who lost their father while in the womb were at increased risk of criminality, alcoholism and mental disease. This study clearly demonstrates that the emotional state of the pregnant mother has more long-term effects on the child than the emotional state of the mother during the year following birth.

Studies of children from unwanted pregnancies provide similar conclusions. At the end of the 1950s a team from Gothenburg, Sweden began a study to investigate from the social-psychiatric viewpoint the lives of children who were born after their mothers had applied for abortion but had the application refused.[13] The 120 people in the study group and 120 people in the control group were first followed up until the age of 21. Then the follow-up was extended to completion of the 35th year. The main conclusion was that the degree of sociability was lower in the group whose mother had unsuccessfully applied for an abortion. The differences were still detectable at the age of thirty-five.

The Prague study is based on a cohort of 220 subjects born to mothers who, between 1961 and 1963, were refused an abortion both on initial request and subsequent appeal.[14] The results of four waves of assessments were published. At age 30, 190 were examined with pair-matched control subjects. As in Sweden, the degree of sociability was lower in the study group.

The design, the objectives and the size of a Finnish study

were different.[15] The 1966 study originally included 11,000 pregnant women. In the sixth or seventh month of pregnancy mothers were asked whether the pregnancy was wanted, mistimed but wanted, or unwanted. The risk of later schizophrenia was significantly raised in the babies born to mothers in the unwanted group compared with the other groups. Schizophrenia can be presented as an impaired capacity to love: the personality is detached from its environment.

Interestingly enough, in spite of enormous technical difficulties, the studies exploring the long-term effects of the emotional states of pregnant women have been prolonged or repeated by several teams. Perhaps they are considered more politically correct than those which detect links with the birth itself.

Summary

When looking at the background of those people who have demonstrated an impaired capacity to love in different ways – whether it be love of oneself or love of others – it seems that the capacity to love is determined, to a great extent, by early experiences during foetal life, and the period around birth.

References

1   Odent, M. *Primal health.* Century Hutchinson, London, 1986.
2   Raine, A., Brennan, P. and Medink, S.A. 'Birth complications combined with early maternal rejection at age 1 year predispose to violent crime at 18 years.' *Arch. Gen. Psychiatry 1994; 51: 984–8.*
3   Salk, L., Lipsitt, L.P. et al. 'Relationship of maternal and perinatal conditions to eventual adolescent suicide.' *Lancet* 16 March 1985: 624–7.
4   Jacobson, B., Nyberg, K. et al. 'Perinatal origin of adult self-destructive behavior.' *Acta. Psychiatr. Scand.* 1987; 76: 364–71.
5   Jacobson, B. and Bygdeman, M. 'Obstetric care and proneness of offspring to suicide as adults: case control study.' *BMJ 1998; 317: 1346–9.*
6   Jacobson, B. and Nyberg, K. 'Opiate addiction in adult offspring through possible imprinting after obstetric treatment.' *BMJ 1990; 301: 1067–70.*

7 Nyberg, K., Buka, S.L. and Lipsitt, L.P. 'Perinatal medication as a potential factor for adult drug abuse in a North American cohort.' *Epidemiology*, 2000; 11(6): 715–16.

8 Cnattingius, S., Hultman, C.M., Dahl, M. and Sparen, P. 'Very preterm birth, birth trauma and the risk of anorexia nervosa among girls.' *Arch. Gen. Psychiatry*, 1999; 56: 634–5.

9 Tinbergen, N. and Tinbergen, A. *Autistic children.* Allen and Unwin, London, 1983.

10 Hattori, R. et al. 'Autistic and developmental disorders after general anaesthesic delivery.' *Lancet* 1 June 1991; 337: 1357–8 (letter).

11 Odent, M. 'Between circular and cul-de-sac epidemiology.' *Lancet*, 2000; 355: 1371.

12 Huttunen, M. and Niskanen, P. 'Prenatal loss of father and psychiatric disorders.' *Arch. Gen. Psychiatry* 1978; 35: 429–31.

13 Forssman, H. and Thuwe, I. 'Continued follow-up study of 120 persons born after refusal of application for therapeutic abortion.' *Acta Psychiatr. Scand.* 1981; 64: 142–9.

14 Kubicka, L., Matejcek, Z. et al. 'Children from unwanted pregnancies in Prague, Czech Republic, revisited at age thirty.' *Acta Psychiatr. Scand.* 1995; 91: 361–9.

15 Myhran, A., Rantakallio, P. et al. 'Unwantedness of a pregnancy and schizophrenia of a child.' *Br. J. Psychiatr.* 1996; 169: 637–40.

5   The Ethnological Approach –
     Comparing Cultures

It would be a mistake not to include the ethnological approach in our overview of the 'scientification of love' – what we can learn by comparing cultures.

Ethnology has established itself as a science by publishing databases. Today its material on pregnancy, childbirth and the first days following birth can be located rapidly.

It is often noted that human societies impose a pattern on the behaviour of human beings at the time of childbirth. It would be more accurate to claim that, one way or another, all cultures disturb the purely physiological process in the period surrounding birth. On the other hand it is obvious that different cultures do not develop in the same direction and at the same degree the human potential for aggression.

The objective of the ethnological approach is to study the main characteristics of different cultures in relation to how babies are born.

Cultures disturb the physiological process by denying the mammalian need for privacy: all the mammals have developed a strategy not to feel observed when giving birth. In many societies (62 per cent in the study by Betsy Lozoff)[1] birth companions try actively to influence the labour: manipulating, kneading, even bouncing on the abdomen or dilating the cervix manually. Most cultures disturb the first contact between mother and baby. The most universal and intriguing way is simply to promote the belief that colostrum is tainted or harmful to the baby – even a substance to be expressed and discarded. Let us recall that, according to modern biological sciences, the colostrum available immediately after birth is precious. Let us also recall the newborn baby's ability to search for the nipple and to find it as early as the first hour following birth. The first contact between mother and baby can also be disturbed through rituals: rushing to cut the cord, bathing, rubbing, tight swaddling, foot binding, 'smoking' the baby, piercing the ears of the little girls, opening the doors in cold countries are examples of such rituals. We might mention many such rituals and beliefs in Western Europe. For example, in Tudor and Stuart England, colostrum was openly regarded as a harmful substance, to be discarded. The mother was not considered to be 'clean' after childbirth until the bloody discharge called lochia had stopped flowing. She was not permitted to breastfeed until after a religious service of purification and thanksgiving called 'churching'.

Learning from Extreme Attitudes

It would take volumes to present a comprehensive study of the characteristics of a great number of cultures in relation to how they challenge the maternal protective instinct during the sensitive period following birth. However, a simple conclusion can be drawn from a rapid overview of the data we have at our disposal: the greater the social need for aggression and an ability to destroy life, the more intrusive the rituals and beliefs have become in the period surrounding birth.

This simple rule can be illustrated by taking as examples some of the more extreme attitudes. In Sparta, in ancient Greece, there was a population of warriors. When a baby boy was born, he was thrown down on the floor. If he managed to survive, he was supposed to become a good warrior.

If disturbing the first contact between mother and baby and promulgating such ideas as the belief that colostrum is bad are so universal, it means that these behaviours carry an evolutionary advantage.[2] To interpret these intriguing paradoxes, one must realise that pre-agricultural peoples became rapidly extinct at the age of anthropological studies. This means that the cultures studied during the twentieth century by anthropologists share the same basic strategies for survival, which are to control nature, and also to dominate other human groups. For such societies it is an advantage to moderate and to control the different aspects of the capacity to love, including love of nature, that is to say, having respect for Mother Earth.

Our interpretation is confirmed by data from a very small number of pre-agricultural peoples that could be studied before becoming extinct, and who had other strategies for survival. Their strategy was to live in perfect harmony with the ecosystem; in such societies it was therefore an advantage to develop this form of love and respect for Mother Earth. The priority in these societies was not to develop the human potential for aggression. This is the case of the Efe Pygmies, who lived in Zaire's Ituri Forest. They had a deeply rooted ecological instinct, and in particular an enormous respect for trees. It seems, according to Jean Pierre Hallet, that they had no rituals or beliefs disturbing the birth process.[3] We know also, thanks to Melvin Konner[4] in particular, about the 'solitary and unaided births' among the African hunters and gatherers, the !Kung San:

> A woman feels the initial stages of labour and makes no comment, leaves the village quietly when birth seems imminent, walks a few hundred yards, finds an area in the shade, clears it, arranges a soft bed of leaves, and gives birth while squatting or lying on her side – on her own.

Obviously the physiological processes were disturbed as little as possible in a human group where the strategy for survival was not to dominate Nature.

The conclusions we can propose from an ethnological approach reinforce these established from other perspectives. The probable long-term consequences of a short period of time surrounding birth are confirmed. The ethnological approach introduces the concept of love of nature and suggests that the relationship with the mother and the relationship with Mother Earth are two aspects of the same phenomenon.

Shaking the Foundations of our Cultures

After comparing cultures we are in a position to propose answers to our previous question regarding politically incorrect

Figure 5.1

Three landmarks in the history of humankind

Year 0   _____
Globalisation   Scientification of love

Ecological awareness

10,000 years   _____ Mastering the human potential
                                 for aggressiveness

Neolithic Revolution

Domination of nature

1 million years ago

Homo Erectus

                _____ Mastery of fire

research. One can understand why those figures who associate their name with both childbirth and the human capacity to love meet major obstacles: they shake the very foundations of our cultures. Since successful ethnic groups – those who are not extinct – are those who had the advantage of reducing and controlling the different aspects of the capacity to love, including love of nature, one can explain the widespread tendency to neutralise, or to outlaw or even to persecute anyone promulgating messages about both the capacity to love and how we are born.

There are similarities between the modern epidemiologists whose computerised data throw a new light on perinatal rituals, beliefs and practices, and an *avant garde* student of human nature such as Wilhelm Reich, who claimed that 'civilisation will start on the day when the well being of newborn babies will prevail over any other consideration'.[5] W. Reich died in jail. His views are similar to those of Frederick Leboyer, who wrote in poetic language about birth and its traces, which are 'everywhere ... in all our human folly, in our madness, our tortures, our prisons, our legends, epics and in myths'.[6] Leboyer's message was neutralised by its corruption into 'the Leboyer method'.

These concepts have much in common with the message transmitted by the legend of Jesus. It is not usual to present Jesus as the one who promoted love after being born in a stable among mammals. The symbolism of this phase of the legend of Jesus has been neutralised for two millennia.

The ethnological approach is also crucial in helping us to realise that only those societies which have been successful at developing their capacity to dominate nature and to dominate other human groups have survived until the end of this millennium. All the other cultural models have disappeared. This is the very time when we realise the urgent need to develop respect for Mother Earth and other facets of the capacity to love. Humanity is at a turning point, when all our deep-rooted perinatal beliefs and rituals are losing their evolutionary advantages.

Now we have reached the age of ecological awareness and scientification of love, humankind must and can shift towards new strategies for survival.

Summary

In most known societies, until now, it has been an advantage to moderate and control the different aspects of the capacity to love, including love of nature, and to develop the human potential for aggressiveness. The greater the need to develop aggression and the ability to destroy life, the more intrusive the rituals and cultural beliefs in the period around birth have become.

References

1   Lozoff, B. 'Birth in non-industrial societies.' In Klaus, M. and Robertson, M.O. *Birth, interaction and attachment*. Johnson and Johnson, Skillman, NJ, 1982.
2   Odent, M. 'Colostrum and civilization.' In *The nature of birth and breastfeeding*. Bergin and Garvey, Westport, CT, 1992.
3   Hallet, J.P. *Pygmy Kitabu*. Random House, New York, 1973.
4   Eaton, S.B., Shostak, M. and Konner, M. *The palaeolithic prescription: a program of diet and exercises and a design for living*. Harper and Row, New York, 1988.
5   Reich, W. *The murder of Christ*. Farrer, Strauss and Giroux, New York, 1953.
6   Leboyer, F. *Pour une naissance sans violence*. Le Seuil, Paris, 1974.

6   Birth Reborn

After fitting together the largest pieces of the broken mirror, it is beyond doubt that the capacity to love is, to a great extent, determined by early experiences and that the period surrounding birth is critical. We have gathered together a number of serious reasons to clarify our understanding of the birth process. That is why, before focusing on smaller pieces that are more difficult to include in the whole picture, I propose a quick overview of birth physiology.

What 'Physiological' Means

We should not confuse the term 'physiological' with the term 'normal'. An attitude or a behaviour can be considered 'normal' in one particular country but not in another. The term 'physiological' does not mean either that 'it should be exactly like that'. What is 'physiological' is a reference point from which we try not to deviate too much. When we deviate beyond a certain limit, there are pathological side effects; and when we must deviate from the physiological reference, we should be constantly aware of the degree of any such deviation. Physiologists explore the body's normal function – what is universal, cross-cultural. After millennia of routine cultural interference in the birth process, it is more necessary than ever to go back to our roots.

I started to understand birth physiology in the early 1960s. In the event of a long and difficult labour we sometimes used a new drug called GBH in English-speaking countries. This substance is, in fact, pretty similar to the brain chemical GABA which, we now know, has the effect of blocking transmission from one brain cell to another. When labouring women were given GBH the activity of what we might call the rational brain was reduced. Following the administration of this drug labouring women were agitated, screaming, behaving as if in a dream ... and the birth was subsequently incredibly fast and easy. The pharmaceutical firm mentioned that GBH had an 'oxytocic effect' so that it would tend to reinforce uterine contractions during labour. I realised that it was not a genuine oxytocic effect and that, actually, it was as if a brake had been released and a flood of hormones had suddenly been liberated. Of course, the behaviour of women screaming without any inhibitions was considered unacceptable in a hospital setting, and there was a lack of data about possible side effects so that, for many reasons, our understanding of the effect of GBH during labour is anecdotal, but from these stories I improved my understanding of the birth process.

The language of modern physiologists can clearly explain what is happening when a woman is giving birth.

With the Language of Physiologists

To give birth a woman needs to release a certain cocktail of hormones. Let us forget the names of these various hormones (oxytocin, endorphins, prolactin, ACTH, catecholamines, etc.). The crucial thing is to realise that they all originate in the same gland – the brain. Today the traditional perceived separation between the nervous system and the endocrine system is obsolete. There is only one network and the brain is also an endocrine gland. But it is not the whole brain which is active as an endocrine gland, only its deepest part. We might say that *when a woman is in labour the most active part of her body is her primitive brain* – those very old structures of the brain (the hypothalamus, pituitary gland, etc.) that we share with all the other mammals. Modern scientific language can also explain that *when there are inhibitions* during the birth process (or any other sexual experience) *they originate in* that other brain, the new brain, *that part of the brain which is so highly developed among humans* – the neocortex.

Physiologists might also interpret a phenomenon which is familiar to midwives and some mothers – or at least to those who have had the experience of unmanaged and unmedicated births. During the birth process there is a period when the mother behaves as if she were 'on another planet', cutting herself off from our everyday world and going on a sort of inner trip. This change in her level of consciousness can be interpreted as *a reduction in the activity of the brain of the intellect*, that is of the neocortex. Birth attendants who understand this essential aspect of the physiology of labour and delivery would not make the mistake of trying to 'bring her back to her senses'. They would readily appreciate that any neocortical stimulation in general, and any stimulation of the intellect in particular, can interfere with the progress of labour.

Giving the Intellect a Rest

From a practical point of view it is useful to review the well-known factors which can stimulate the human neocortex: *language*, particularly rational language is one such factor. Imagine a woman in hard labour, and already 'on another planet'. She dares to scream out; she dares to do things she would never do otherwise; she has forgotten about what she has been taught or read in books; and then she finds herself in the unexpected position of having to respond to someone who has come into the room and asked her for her post code! *Bright light* is another factor which will stimulate the human neocortex. Electroencephalographers know that the trace can be influenced by visual stimulation.

A *feeling of being observed* is a type of neocortical stimulation. The physiological response to the presence of an observer has been scientifically studied. In fact, it is common knowledge that we all feel different when we know we are being observed. In other words, privacy is a factor which facilitates the reduction of neocortical control. It is ironic that all non-human mammals, whose neocortex is not as developed as ours, have a strategy for giving birth in privacy – those who are normally active during night, like rats, tend to give birth during the day, and conversely others, like horses, who are active during the day, tend to give birth at night. Goats separate from the herd and wild goats give birth in the most inaccessible mountain areas. Our close relatives the chimpanzees also move away from the group.

Any situation likely to trigger a release of hormones of the adrenaline family also tends to stimulate the neocortex and to inhibit the birth process as a result. This means that a labouring woman first needs to feel secure. This *feeling of security* is a prerequisite for the changing level of consciousness which characterises the birth process. All over the world and down throughout the ages most women have adopted a similar strategy to feel secure when giving birth, and so maintaining a low level of adrenaline for as long as possible. They have made sure that their own mother was at hand, or a substitute for their mother in the framework of the extended family, or a mothering and experienced woman belonging to the community ... a substitute for their own mother, i.e. a midwife. An authentic midwife is a mother figure. The mother is the prototype of the person with whom one feels secure, without feeling observed and judged.

If we consider mammals in general it is an advantage for the survival of the species that labour cannot establish itself as long as the female feels threatened (so she is ready to fight or run away from a predator if necessary). While a low level of adrenaline hormones is a prerequisite for the initiation of real labour and for an easy first stage, the role of adrenaline during labour is actually a complex one and a rush of adrenaline is part of the spectacular hormonal release of the minutes preceding birth.

Some women can reach such a peak of hormone secretion and achieve such a reduction of their neocortical activity that they compare the very last seconds of the delivery to an orgasm. In the early 1980s a well-known BBC TV presenter visited our hospital in France. During her visit a woman gave birth to her first baby (a footling breech presentation). An hour after the birth the presenter asked the young mother what she felt when the baby arrived. Her spontaneous reply was 'It was like an orgasm.' Millions of British TV viewers were witnesses.

A Cultural Misunderstanding

The language of physiologists helps us to evaluate the current collective cultural misunderstanding of the birth process. This misunderstanding is transmitted via non-verbal messages. In books about childbirth, for example, it is commonplace to see a picture of a woman in labour with two or three people at her side, watching her. Such messages are reinforced by words. The sort of vocabulary which is often used to describe the birth attendant is suggestive of a widespread misinterpretation of the birth process and of the original role of the midwife. When considering the birth process from the perspective of physiologists, it is clear that a labouring woman needs first to feel secure and that a midwife is originally a protector, a mother-figure, the mother being the prototype of the sort of person with whom one feels secure. However, the words qualifying the birth attendant, particularly in the USA, where midwives are reappearing after a prolonged absence, are obviously inappropriate. Many words suggest that the birth attendant is an active helper or guide. The word 'coach', for example, which has been popular in the USA, translates and transmits a deep misunderstanding of birth physiology. The word 'support' is probably the most misleading term because it is overused.[1] It suggests that a woman cannot give birth unless some kind of energy is fed in by somebody else. I need an analogy to express what I feel whenever I read or hear the word 'support' with reference to childbirth. Imagine a young boy who cannot fall asleep without the presence of his mummy. You would never claim that this child needs a 'support person' to fall asleep. The sleeping process is better understood than the birth process. In both cases it is necessary to feel secure in order to reduce the activity of the intellect. In medical textbooks, the word 'labour' is more often than not associated with the word 'management' – how can you manage an involuntary process?

The surprise many doctors expressed when reading the results of serious statistical studies is another sign of a widespread misconception of the physiological process. A dozen studies were designed to evaluate the ratio of risks to benefits in using continuous electronic foetal monitoring during labour as opposed to listening to the baby's heart beats now and then. Researchers everywhere have agreed that the only constant and significant effect of electronic monitoring on birth statistics is to increase the rate of caesarean sections. Initially doctors responded to this finding by saying there was clearly a need to re-learn how to interpret the graph correctly, and it became commonplace to claim that birth attendants should be better educated in a more scientific fashion. Subsequently, the reaction focused on a need to explore more sophisticated techniques of continuous monitoring. Professionals who share this popular misconception about the physiology of birth are not really best placed to reconsider the very principle of continuous monitoring, nor can they imagine that the mere fact that a woman knows that her body functions are being continuously monitored might itself represent a stimulant of her neocortex which could make the birth more difficult and therefore more dangerous. In other words, electronic foetal monitoring is an effective way to detect certain cases of foetal distress immediately, but it is also itself a cause of foetal distress and, as a result, the risks of the procedure outweigh the benefits.

Our overview of birth physiology is voluntarily and inevitably simplistic. It is based on a combination of scientifically established facts and empirical knowledge. For example, the inhibitory effects of adrenaline may be considered as scientifically established,[2] whereas the effects of asking a labouring woman her post code is empirical knowledge. The opposition between the new brain and the old brain is a simplified and convenient way to concentrate on essentials. If there was a non-invasive way to scan the brain of a labouring woman, we might be in for a few surprises.

Summary

After enumerating some of the reasons why we should clarify our understanding of the birth process, we offer an overview of birth physiology. This is the best way to rediscover the basic needs of women in labour. During the birth process the active part of the body is the primitive part of the brain, which functions as a gland, releasing hormones. When inhibitions arise they originate in the part of the brain which is so highly developed in humans – the neocortex. Reduced neocortical activity – as if 'going to another planet' – is a most important aspect of birth physiology from a practical point of view. Any stimulation of the mother's neocortex – talking to her rationally, surrounding her with bright lights, making her feel observed, insecure or otherwise stimulating her release of adrenalin – tends to inhibit the birth process.

References

1 Odent, M. 'Why laboring women don't need support.' *Mothering* 1996; 80: 46–51.
2 Lederman, R.P., Lederman, E., Work, B.A. and McCann, D.S. 'The relationship of maternal anxiety, plasma catecholamines and plasma cortisol to progress in labor.' *Am. J. Obstet. Gynecol.* 1978; 132: 495.

7   Sexuality as a Whole

Today it is artificial to study the episodes that are essential for the survival of the species in isolation. The same hormones are involved and similar patterns of behaviour are reproduced. Sexual intercourse, childbirth and lactation can be inhibited by the same neocortical centres – we might say the same neocortical brakes. In other words modern physiologists view sexuality as a whole.

Love Hormones in the Limelight

Oxytocin is one of the main hormones involved in different aspects of male and female sexuality. It is secreted by a primitive structure of the brain called the hypothalamus, then sequestered in the posterior pituitary gland, and suddenly pulses into the bloodstream in specific circumstances in a discontinuous fashion.

We focused on oxytocin as a hormone capable of inducing maternal behaviour in the hour following birth. It is also released during intercourse by both partners. Its role during sexual arousal and orgasm has only recently come to light. Of course, there have been countless experiments with oxytocin on rats and other animals.[1,2] For example, when domestic fowl and pigeons are injected with oxytocin the majority will start waltzing, grabbing each others' combs, mounting and mating within a minute of the injection. For several decades oxytocin has been used to get animals in captivity to mate. We now have scientific studies of oxytocin levels during orgasm among humans. Marie Carmichael's team from Stanford University in California has published a study in which oxytocin levels among men and women during masturbation and orgasm were measured in blood samples collected continuously via indwelling venous catheters.[3] Levels during self-stimulation before orgasm were higher amongst women than men. Indeed, they were higher during the second phase of the menstrual cycle than during the first phase. During orgasm, women had higher levels of oxytocin than men, and multi-orgasmic women reached a higher peak during the second orgasm.

Oxytocin plays a direct role in reproduction. During male orgasm the release of oxytocin helps to induce contractions of the prostate and seminal vesicles.[4] During female orgasm the immediate effect of the release of oxytocin is to induce uterine contractions which help the transportation of the sperm towards the egg. This was shown as early as 1961 by two American surgeons during a gynaecological operation.[5] Before making the abdominal incision they introduced particles of carbon into the woman's vagina close to the cervix and, at the same time, gave her an injection of oxytocin. Later they found particles of carbon in her fallopian tubes.

These scientific data imply an absolutely new vision of female orgasm. Anthropologists such as Margaret Mead[6] and Donald Symons noticed that many societies have totally ignored female orgasm. They proposed an explanation: female orgasm has no reproductive function. At the same stage in the history of the biological sciences, Wilhelm Reich also had difficulty accounting for the reproductive role of female orgasm.[7]

We have also learned more about the release of oxytocin during lactation. It has been shown recently that as soon as the mother receives the signal given by her hungry baby her level of oxytocin increases[8] – a phenomenon similar to the sexual arousal which frequently precedes any skin stimulation. As the baby sucks the level of oxytocin released by the mother is about the same as during orgasm – another parallel between these two events in sexual life.[9]

During ultrasound scans it has been noticed that, from as early as 27 weeks' gestation, baby boys often have an erection while sucking their thumbs.[10] This means that they can already release oxytocin. By releasing its own oxytocin the foetus could contribute to the onset of labour. It is as if it were possible for human beings to train themselves from very early on to release their love hormone.

If we add that sharing a meal with companions has also been found to increase our level of oxytocin, we can undoubtedly conclude that there is an altruistic hormone, a hormone of love.[11]

The study of how oxytocin is released appears to be a promising avenue of research. It seems that oxytocin is more effective when released rhythmically with a fast succession of pulsations. It is now possible to measure the rhythmicity – the pulsatility – of oxytocin release. A Swedish team demonstrated that during a breastfeeding session two days after the birth, the maternal release of oxytocin is less pulsatile after emergency caesarean birth than after spontaneous vaginal delivery.[12] Furthermore there is a correlation between the way oxytocin is released two days after birth and the eventual duration of breastfeeding. This is a significant example of the many connections between birth physiology and the physiology of lactation.

The hormone of love is always part of a complex hormonal balance. When there is a sudden release of oxytocin, the need to love can be directed in different ways according to the hormonal balance. That is why there are different sorts of love. When there is a high level of prolactin, the tendency is to direct the effects of the love hormone toward babies. Prolactin is well known as the hormone necessary to initiate and sustain lactation. In fact it is an ancient hormone on the evolutionary scale, serving multiple roles in mediating the care of the offspring, from nest building, for example, up to the aggressive defensive behaviour typical of lactating mothers.[13, 14]

Prolactin is not only the mothering hormone but also acts to reduce sexual desire and the ability to conceive. Generally speaking, lactating mammals are not receptive to the male. Their capacity to love is almost exclusively directed towards their babies. In most known traditional societies, where babies were breastfed for several years before weaning, breastfeeding and sexual intercourse were considered incompatible. It is only relatively recently in the history of humankind, since strict lifelong monogamy became the norm, that it has been necessary for women to resume genital sexual activity shortly after giving birth, and there has been a tendency to curtail the period of breastfeeding or to find substitutes for the mother's milk. The duration of breastfeeding and family structures are two interrelated topics.

While a high level of prolactin is associated with parental love, a low level goes hand in hand with genital love. In a group of primates the dominant male – the most sexually active – has the lowest level of prolactin, while those who are subordinate and obedient have higher levels. Their sexual desire is reduced.

A Reward System

Oxytocin is not the only hormone released during all episodes of our sexual life. While oxytocin is the altruistic hormone and prolactin the mothering hormone, endorphins represent our reward system. Each time we mammals do something that benefits the survival of the species, we are rewarded by the secretion of these morphine-like substances.[15] They are both hormones of pleasure and natural pain killers. All mammals protect themselves during the birth process by increasing their level of endorphins. This is the beginning of a long chain reaction: 'Beta-endorphins' release prolactin;[16, 17] in other words we cannot dissociate birth and the initiation of lactation. Furthermore, prolactin is one of the hormones which puts the finishing touch to the maturation of the baby's lungs.

I mentioned that during the birth process the foetus is also increasing its own level of endorphins so that, in the few minutes following birth, both mother and baby are still under the effects of opiates. This is the beginning of a dependency – a strong attachment.

Copulation is also necessary for the survival of the species. The endorphins released during copulation among different species of mammals is well documented. For example, beta endorphin levels in the blood of male hamsters after their fifth ejaculation were found to be 86 times higher than those of control animals. In simple terms, the incentive for mammalian love-making is the reward of the pleasure we experience.

Among humans, it is also well understood that during intercourse partners release high levels of endorphins. Some migraine sufferers know that intercourse is a natural remedy for their headache. One can understand that when sexual partners are close to each other and impregnated with opiates a sort of dependency is created following a similar model to the attachment between mother and baby. One cannot study intercourse without studying the birth process in parallel.

Lactation is also necessary for the survival of mammals, so it is not surprising that the same reward system is involved. When a woman is breastfeeding her level of beta endorphins peaks after 20 minutes. The baby is also rewarded – there are endorphins in human milk. That is why, after being breastfed, babies sometimes behave and look as if they are in ecstasy.

Similar Physiological Brakes

Another aspect common to the different episodes of sexual life is that they are inhibited by the hormones of the adrenaline family. These are the emergency hormones which give us the energy to protect ourselves by fighting or running away. It is as if there were priorities in terms of survival of the species. That is why labour cannot progress when the mother is scared. That is why people would not make love if their house was on fire, and a farmer knows that if a cow is frightened she cannot give milk. More generally speaking, the different episodes of sexual life are under the control of the same brakes that are applied from the neocortical inhibitory centres. That is the origin of specifically human difficulties: low sex drive, difficult births and difficulties in breastfeeding are common in our species. In fact, other mammals – particularly the primates – also have a cortical brake that is just less powerful than ours. In 1939 a team from Chicago published the effects of surgical intervention on male monkeys (operations that would not be ethically tolerable today). They removed temporal lobes, and found that 3 to 6 months after the operation the monkeys appeared 'hypersexed', not only when with other animals, but also when alone.[18]

Similar Scenarios

As we can see, not only are the same hormones involved in these different episodes of sexual life, but the same patterns, the same sort of scenarios are reproduced. The final phase of each sexual event is always an 'ejection reflex' and terms such as 'sperm ejection reflex', 'foetus ejection reflex', 'milk ejection reflex' are highly suggestive of this likeness. I adopted the term 'foetus ejection reflex' (which had been proposed previously by the American scientist Niles Newton in the context of non-human mammals) to refer to the very last contractions before birth among humans, when the whole process has been undisturbed and unguided.[19, 20] This is a very short phase when, paradoxically, strong and effective contractions are associated with a rush of adrenaline so that the mother has a tendency to be alert when the baby is born. This reflex is almost unknown in hospital delivery rooms, and even at home births it is inhibited if another person takes on the role of 'coach', 'guide', 'helper', 'support person' or 'observer'.

An Interaction Between Two Individuals

In the special context of the nuclear family, there is another common point between the different episodes of sexual life that needs to be stressed and clarified. This common point is obvious where the mammals in general are concerned, including human beings in any other culture than our own. I mean that any sexual episode which is essential for reproduction is an interaction between two individuals. It seems indisputable from a physiological perspective that intercourse is an event between two partners. It is apparently indisputable that lactation is an interaction between mother and baby. However, in the context of the nuclear family, since the advent of a generation of working women and career women, and whilst 'humanised' milk formulas remain easily available, some have proposed a futuristic vision of baby-feeding as an activity involving the mother and the father equally. Such behaviour and theories are, in fact, adaptations to an unprecedented situation and are deviations from the physiological model. When looking at the whole period surrounding birth from the perspective of physiologists, it seems obvious that once more only two individuals are directly interacting. The foetus participates in the initiation of labour, sending messages (particularly from her newly mature lungs and kidneys) via chemical mediators that stimulate the synthesis of the appropriate sorts of prostaglandins. During the birth process both mother and baby reach very specific hormonal balances at the same time, and all these hormones have a particular role to play during the hour following birth before they are eliminated. Just after the birth, if the interaction between mother and baby is disturbed by a third person, the mother will not release a sufficiently high level of oxytocin and delivery of the placenta will be complicated. From the hormonal point of view, the birth itself and the hour following appear once more to be a series of interactions between two individuals.

It is no different if we take into account the bacteriological point of view. At birth, a baby is germ-free. Some hours later there are billions of germs covering its mucous membranes. The question is – which germs will be the first to colonise the baby's body? Bacteriologists know that the winners of the race will be the rulers of the territory. The germ environment of the mother is already familiar and friendly from the perspective of the newborn because mother and baby share the same antibodies (IgG). In other words, from a bacteriological point of view, the newborn human baby urgently needs to be in contact with only one person – her mother. If we add that early consumption of colostrum will help establish an ideal gut flora there is no doubt that, from a bacteriological point of view, the hour following birth continues to be a vital interaction between two people.

This is a point that needs to be emphasised. Today there is a tendency to illustrate books about childbirth with pictures of the 'couple giving birth'. More mention is made of the 'bonding' between father and baby as a phenomenon comparable and even identical to the bonding between mother and baby. This can be dangerous from a short-term point of view. I am convinced that most cases of post-partum haemorrhage and difficult deliveries of the placenta occur because the mother has been distracted at a time when she should have nothing else to do other than look at her baby and feel the baby's skin close to her body. From a long-term point of view it might be dangerous to rush the traditionally slower and more gradual process of attachment between father and child. It seems that in most traditional societies, and among our closely related cousins the chimpanzees, the beginnings of the attachment between male adult and baby is, to a certain extent, indirect, via the attachment to the mother.

Practical Implications

This integrated vision of sexual life inspired by modern biological sciences has practical implications. It explains why, when a cultural milieu interferes routinely in one particular episode of sexual life, it is in fact our entire sexuality at a cultural level which is influenced. It also helps us to interpret anthropological data suggesting that in societies where genital sexuality is highly repressed, women may not be capable of having easy births.

Summary

During intercourse, childbirth and lactation, two groups of hormones play a pre-eminent role – the altruistic hormone oxytocin, and the endorphins which can be considered to be our 'reward system'. An integrated vision of sexual life inspired by modern biological sciences has practical implications.

References

1   Arletti, R., Bazzani, M., Castelli, M. and Bertoline, A. 'Oxytocin improves copulatory behavior in rats.' *Hormones and Behavior* 1985; 19: 14–20.
2   McNeilly, A.S. and Ducker, H.A. 'Blood levels of oxytocin in the female goat during coitus and in response to stimuli associated with mating.' *J. Endocrinol.* 1972; 54: 399–406.

3 Carmichael, M.S., Humbert, R. et al. 'Plasma oxytocin increases in the human sexual response.' *J. Clin. Endocrinol. and Metab.* 1987; 64; 1: 27–31.

4 Sharaf, H., Foda, H.D., Said, S.I. and Bodansky, M. 'Oxytocin and related peptides elicit contractions of prostate and seminal vesicle.' In Pedersen, C.A. et al., eds *Oxytocin in maternal, sexual and social behavior. Annals of the New York Academy of Science* 1992; 652: 474–7.

5 Egli, C.E. and Newton, M. 'Transport of carbon particles in the human female reproductive tract.' *Fertility and Sterility* 1961; 12: 151–5.

6 Mead, Margaret. *Male and female.* William Morrow, New York, 1948.

7 Reich, W. *The function of the orgasm.* Panther Books, London, 1968.

8 McNeilly, A.S., Robinson, I.C. et al. 'Release of oxytocin and prolactin in response to suckling.' *BMJ* 1983; 286: 257–9.

9 Leake, R.D., Water, C.B. et al. 'Oxytocin and prolactin responses in long-term breastfeeding.' *Obstet. Gynecol.* 1983; 62: 565.

10 Hitchcock, D.A., Stuphen, J.H. and Scholly, T.A. 'Demonstration of fetal penile erection in utero.' *Perinatology-Neonatology* May/June 1980: 59–60.

11 Newton, N. and Modahl, C. 'Oxytocin-psychoactive hormone of love and breastfeeding.' In *The free woman.* Parthenon, Carnforth, Lancs.,1989, 343–50.

12 Nissen, E., Uvnas-Moberg, K. et al. 'Different patterns of oxytocin, prolactin but not cortisol release during breastfeeding in women delivered by caesarean section or by the vaginal route.' *Early Human Development* 1996; 45: 103–18.

13 Herbert, J. 'Hormones and behavior.' *Proc. Royal Society,* London, Series B. Biological Sciences 1977; 199: 425–3.

14 Uvnas-Moberg, K. 'Hormone release in relation to physiological and psychological changes in pregnant and breastfeeding women.' In *The free woman.* Parthenon, Carnforth, Lancs., 1989: 316–25.

15 Murphy, M.D., Bowie, D. and Pert, D. 'Copulation elevates beta-endorphins in the hamster.' *Soc. Neurosci. Abstr.* 1979; 5: 470.

16 Franceschini, R., Venturini, P.L. et al. 'Plasma beta-endorphins concentrations during suckling in lactating women.' *Brit. J. Obstet. Gynaecol.* 1989; 96: 711–13.

17 Schulz, S.C., Wagner R., et al. 'Prolactin response to beta-endorphin in man.' *Life Sci. 1980; 27: 1735–41.*

18 Kluver, H. and Bucy, P.C. 'Preliminary analysis of functions of the temporal lobes in monkeys.' *Arch. Neurology and Psychiatr.* 1939; 42; 6: 979–1000.
19 Odent, M. 'The fetus ejection reflex.' *Birth* 1987; 14: 104–5.
20 Newton, N. 'The fetus ejection reflex revisited.' *Birth* 1987; 14: 106–8.

8   Sexual Attractiveness

Before the 1990s, at an early stage of the scientification of love, the measurement of sexual appeal was not a subject introduced in the respectable scientific or medical journals. At that time it was difficult to predict that the following formula, where y represents a measure of male attractiveness for women, would be publishable in the *Lancet*:

$$y = 2.776 \, x1 - 0.0607 \, x2 - 13.007 \, x3 - 16.796$$

(the x represents such criteria as 'body mass index', 'waist:chest ratio', and 'waist:hip ratio').[1]

Today I do not hesitate to present sexual attractiveness among humans as a well-polished piece of the broken mirror. Several factors have been investigated to determine masculine and feminine attributes of sexual attractiveness, in particular simple physical characteristics indicative of body shape and facial shape.

Body Shape and Body Size

The formula we mentioned was extracted from an article which is representative of this new generation of scientific investigation. Thirty female students aged 20 were asked to rate coloured pictures of men in front view. For each man the authors had evaluated the weight in relation to height ('body mass index'), the upper body shape ('waist:chest ratio'), and the lower body shape ('waist:hip ratio'). The statisticians took all the usual precautions such as choosing 50 pictures in a series of 214 to make sure that there was an appropriate 'range of variation'. Furthermore the images were presented in random order, and the students saw the full set of images before they rated them one by one. According to this study there is a strong correlation between the waist:chest ratio and attractiveness. The results show that a woman's ratings of male attractiveness can be explained by simple physical characteristics. Women prefer men whose torso has an 'inverted triangle' shape, that is to say a narrow waist and a broad chest and shoulders. This is a shape consistent with physical strength and muscle development in the upper body. The body mass index is comparatively unimportant.

By contrast a similar study of female sexual attractiveness for men came to the conclusion that the most important factor is the body mass index.[2] It is not the ratio of the width of the waist to the width of the hips. There is an optimal weight in relation to height for a maximum sexual attractiveness. Such results contradict the preconceived idea that a curvaceous body, which corresponds to the optimal fat distribution for high fertility, is highly attractive. It seems that the importance of the weight:hip ratio had been overestimated in preliminary enquiries. We must underline that in these studies of sexual attractiveness in relation to body shape or body size the heads of the images were obscured.

Facial Shape and Smiling Faces

The influence of facial features on sexual attractiveness must also be taken into consideration. The effects of facial asymmetry have been studied by Karl Grammer, from the University of Vienna. He generated computer images of men's and women's faces.[3] The men and women rated faces of the opposite sex. The main conclusion is that facial asymmetry has a negative influence. The role of facial asymmetry in human sexual selection inspires questions about the genetic and environmental factors which are at the roots of the deviation from bilateral facial symmetry. A team from the University of Michigan assessed the relationship between facial asymmetry and health among 101 students.[4] According to this study facial asymmetry may signal psychological, emotional and physiological distress. This can help with interpreting the adaptive role of facial asymmetry in human sexual selection.

Smiling is a specifically human trait. The attractiveness of the smile has been evaluated by a team of prosthodontists in South Korea.[5] In an attractive smile, the full shape of the maxillary anterior teeth was shown between the upper and lower lip, the upper lip curved upward or was straight, the maxillary anterior incisal curve was parallel to the lower lip, and teeth were displayed to the first molar. This study included an assessment of the personality of the subjects by means of a 16-item personality factor questionnaire. The main conclusion is that an attractive smile is closely related to personality traits such as warmth, calmness, extroversion and low anxiety.

Odours and Pheromones

Old texts and historical anecdotes indicate that the role of odours in sexual attractiveness has been empirical knowledge for a long time in a great variety of cultural contexts. There is an erotic connotation associated with the fragrance attested by the Song of Songs, the wedding liturgy of King David, which says 'while the king was on his couch my nard gave forth his fragrance'. A message from Napoleon to Josephine is highly significant: 'I'll arrive in Paris tomorrow evening, don't wash.'

The roles of odours and of the sense of smell in sexual attractiveness have been recently evaluated with scientific methods. According to Karl Grammer, women tend to prefer the smell of men with an immune system that is different from their own. Today great importance is attached to 'pheromones', that is to say substances excreted externally by the body. Although they have no obvious odour they are picked up by the vomerine receptors inside the nose. Karl Grammer made a study of the effects on men of vaginal pheromones known as copulins. His research also showed that the male pheromone androsterone, found in underarm sweat, is attractive for women when they are ovulating and at their most fertile.[6] Our current knowledge of the role of pheromones in sexual attractiveness has been reinforced by experiments conducted at the Athena Institute for Women's Wellness Research, in Pennsylvania.[7] These experiments tested whether synthesised human male pheromones increase the sociosexual behaviour of men. An 8-week double-blind placebo-controlled trial tested a pheromone 'designed to improve the romance in their lives'. Each subject kept daily records for six sociosexual behaviours (petting/kissing, formal dates, informal dates, sleeping next to a romantic partner, sexual intercourse and masturbation) and faxed them each week. Among pheromone users there was a significant increase in male sociosexual behaviours in which a woman's sexual interest and cooperation plays a role, but not in male masturbation which involves only the man.

When referring to the studies of the effects of odours, we go beyond the issue of sexual attractiveness by introducing the issue of personalised sexual attraction. In spite of this new generation of scientific studies, many aspects of sexual attraction and sexual preference remain mysterious. It is well known that sexual attraction is reinforced by a certain degree of mystery. Erotic art suggests without being explicit. Now we feel ready to introduce the complex issue of romantic love.

Summary

Masculine and feminine attributes of sexual attractiveness are currently investigated with scientific methods: body shape and body size, facial asymmetry, smile, chemicals perceived by the sense of smell.

References

1 Maisey, D.S., Vale, E.L.E., Cornelissen, P.L. and Tovee, M.J. 'Characteristics of male attractiveness for women.' *Lancet* 1999; 353: 1500.

2 Tovee, M.J., Reinhardt, S., Emery, J.L. and Cornelissen, P.L. 'Optimal BMI = maximum sexual attractiveness.' *Lancet* 1998; 352: 548.

3 Grammer, K. and Thornhill, R. 'Human (*Homo Sapiens*) facial attractiveness and sexual selection: the role of symmetry and averageness.' *J. Comp. Psychol.* 1994; 108; 3: 233–42.

4 Shackelford, T.K. and Larsen, R.J. 'Facial asymmetry as an indicator of psychological, emotional and physiological distress.' *J. Pers. Soc. Psychol.* 1997; 72; 2: 456–66.

5 Dong, J.K., Jin, T.H., Cho, H.W. and Oh, S.C. 'The aesthetics of smile: a review of some recent studies.' *Int. J. Prosthodont.* 999; 12; 1: 9–19.

6 Grammer, K. and Julte, A. 'Battle of odours: significance of pheromones for human reproduction' (article in German). *Gynakol. Geburtshilfliche Rundsch* 1997; 37; 3: 150–3.

7 Cutler, W.B., Friedmann, E. and McCoy, N.L. 'Pheromonal influences on sociosexual behaviour in men.' *Arch. Sex. Behav.* 1998; 27;1: 1–13.

9   The Physiology of Romantic Love

In the age of the scientification of love, even the physiology of romance can be studied. The difficulties are obvious. Physiology makes us think of animal models and animal experiments. That is why the association of the terms 'physiology' and 'romantic love' immediately produces the 'species-ist' reaction that non-human mammals are inadequate to explore the brain chemistry of Tristan and Isolde, or Romeo and Juliet. The first difficulty stems from the fact that most mammals are promiscuous or polygamous by nature.

Animal Models

However, scientists have found animal models to study 'pair bonding' and 'partner preference'. There are some mammals – including primates – who are more monogamous than humans. This is the case of the gibbons, small man-like apes that live in the Indo-Malayan forests. When compared with other apes – including humans – it appears that their monogamy is associated with the fact that the body size of the male is no bigger than the female, and the penis is comparatively smaller than in other species of primates. Also, compared with the polygynic orangutan and gorilla, and with the promiscuous chimpanzee, the gibbon has a very low sex drive. It has a selective libido, directed towards only one sexual partner. Perhaps, one day, physiologists will do an in-depth comparative study of the brain chemistry of gibbons in order to throw light on the mysterious phenomenon of selective libido. Up to now, their favourite species for this sort of research has been a mouse-like rodent known as the prairie vole. Lowell Getz of the University of Illinois, at Urbana-Champaign, found by chance that these rodents are monogamous, while their close cousins the montana voles exhibit a more promiscuous dating style. Getz discovered that 75 per cent of these pairs broke up only when a mate died, and that only rarely would a male prairie vole abandon his mate.

Research inspired by these observations indicates that oxytocin and vasopressin – two related hormones released by the posterior pituitary gland – probably play an important role in the different aspects of monogamous behaviour.[1] Preferring one particular sexual partner, protecting one's mate and sharing parenting tasks with the partner are characteristics almost never seen among promiscuous and polygamous mammals. Shapiro and Insel compared the brain receptors of the monogamous prairie vole and the polygamous Montana vole.[2] They found obvious differences when looking at the distribution of the brain receptors to oxytocin. Williams et al. examined the effects of cohabitation, sexual experience and the role of oxytocin in the development of partner preference among prairie voles.[3] The results of their experiments indicate that females, given at least 24 hours of cohabitation with a male, develop a preference for the familiar partner. Mating is not essential for the development of partner preferences, but clearly facilitates the onset of preference. Females who were given only 6 hours of cohabitation show partner preference only if they mated or if they were injected with oxytocin in their cerebral ventricles.

More precise data about the hormonal basis of pair bonding among prairie voles were provided recently by a team from Atlanta, Georgia.[4] They completed the previous experiments by analysing the effects of injections in the cerebral ventricles of either oxytocin or vasopressin on female and male voles. They also studied the effects of drugs which inhibit the effects of either oxytocin or vasopressin. It seems that oxytocin plays a major role in partner preference formation in female prairie voles, whereas vasopressin plays a major role in males. Vasopressin, which is the 'water retention hormone', is a parent hormone of oxytocin. Both are released by the posterior pituitary gland. From a chemical point of view, there are only minor differences between these two 'nonapeptides'. They have a common ancestor in the evolutionary process.[5] This common ancestor is not purely theoretical: it has been identified in such a gastropod mollusc as *Lymnaea Stagnalis*.

The Universality of Romantic Love

The evolutionary advantage of pair-bonding among humans seems obvious at first. Human beings are born in a stage of exceptional immaturity and the mother cannot rear the child by herself insofar as she then would have to obtain her own food and this interferes with the care of her young. But most human cultures adapted to these specifically human needs in the framework of a great variety of extended families. Strict monogamy leading to the nuclear family is quite recent in the history of humankind. What seems to be specific to human beings is the process of infatuation, that is to say the state of 'falling in love'.

Anthropologists are now convinced that romantic love is universal and not a product of particular cultures such as the western medieval culture. A survey presented at a session of the American Anthropological Association in 1992 found romantic love in 147 cultures out of 166. What of the other 19? According to the organisers of the session, it is probable that the anthropologists were just unable to recognise different variations of romantic behaviour particular to these rare cultures.

Today a naturally occurring amphetamine substance called phenylethylamine (PEA) is supposed to play a key role as a stimulant for romantic and other kinds of excitement.[6] After a time the brain tends to become less sensitive to the effect of PEA, or the level of PEA begins to drop. It is likely that the different systems of neurotransmitters (chemicals that establish connections between nerve cells) are involved in the process of infatuation. According to the preliminary studies of Donatella Marazziti, of the University of Pisa, the serotonin level is low during the early romantic phase of a love relationship[7] – as low as among those who suffer from 'obsessive compulsive disorders', that is to say, people who constantly repeat, in exactly the same sequence, different sorts of daily rituals (for example, polishing every day their four pairs of shoes at the same time and in exactly the same order). Interestingly, the ethologist Konrad Lorenz hypothesised that human obsessive compulsive behaviour has its roots in animal sexual rituals such as, among birds, nest building or courtship. This series of analogies suggests that the state of 'falling in love' is 'hard-wired' into the human brain.

The period of infatuation seems to be between 18 months and 3 years among many couples. The period of infatuation may be followed by a process of attachment. An interpretation of attachment between sexual partners can be proposed in the current scientific context.

There are many reasons to suspect that endorphins play a role in the attachment between sexual partners – pretty similar to their role in the attachment between mother and baby during the hour following birth. This is a reason why the physiology of birth and the physiology of intercourse should not be studied separately. Copulation among humans meets all the conditions to facilitate the initiation of a state of dependency between the two partners while they release their natural opiates. There is usually a large surface of skin to skin contact between them. The sexual act usually lasts much longer than among our close cousins the chimpanzees (whose intromission, thrusting and ejaculation normally takes 10 to 15 seconds). Moreover, human beings have intense orgasmic reactions, probably correlated with the release of high levels of opiates. Another interesting human female trait is multiple orgasm. The capacity of some women to reach multiple orgasm suggests that female orgasm has many roles to play in human reproduction, and not only to facilitate the transportation of the sperm to the egg. First, it signals satisfaction to the male, who is gratified, and perhaps less inclined to seek sex elsewhere. This signal contributes towards cementing a relationship with her partner. Also orgasm satiates a woman so that she tends to remain lying down; hence, the sperm is less likely to flow out of the vagina. Of course physiologists cannot have enough information to understand the complexity of human behaviour and human emotions, but they give some interesting clues.

Love-Sickness

Among humans it has been easier, until now, to study the other side of the coin – that is to say the side effects of the capacity to 'fall in love'. It is because humans have a tendency for pair-bonding that they can also experience 'love-sickness' when there is uncertainty about mutual love, or in the case of unrequited love. This can lead to a great variety of syndromes, from chronic fatigue up to major depression. Love-sickness has been interpreted as a sort of withdrawal syndrome, of craving for neurotransmitters such as PEA. This is not a purely theoretical consideration since one possible approach to treat perpetually love-sick people is to give them anti-depressant drugs that boost the levels of PEA and other transmitters like norepinephrine.

Today the rational approach of science has the power to penetrate the mysteries of romantic love. If scientists are ambitious enough, they will challenge the statement of Pascal: 'Le coeur a ses raisons que la raison ne connait pas.'

Summary

Romantic love is universal and not a product of one particular culture. It can be studied from a number of complementary perspectives. A study of the other side of the coin – love-sickness – can facilitate our understanding of the nature of romantic love.

References

1 Carter, C.S. and Getz, L.L. 'Social and hormonal determinants of reproductive patterns in the prairie vole.' In Gilles, R. and Belthaz-art, J. eds *Neurobiology*. Springer-Verlag, Berlin, 1985: 18–36.

2 Shapiro, L.E. and Insel, T.R. 'Oxytocin receptor distribution reflects social organization in monogamous and polygamous voles.' In Pedersen, C.A. et al. eds *Oxytocin in maternal, sexual and social behaviors. Annals of the New York Academy of Sciences* 1992; 652: 448–51.

3 Williams, J.R. and Carter, C.S. 'Partner preference development in female prairie voles is facilitated by mating or the central infusion of oxytocin.' In Pedersen, C.A. et al. eds *Oxytocin in maternal sexual and social behavior. Annals of the New York Academy of Sciences* 1992; 652: 487–9.

4   Insel, T.R., Winslow, J.T., Wang, Z. and Young, L.J. 'Oxytocin,
    vasopressin, and the neuroendocrine basis of pair bond formation.'
    Adv. Exp. Med. Biol. 1998; 449: 215–24.
5   Van Kesteren, R.E., Smit, A.B., Dirks, R.W. et al. 'Evolution of the
    vasopressin/oxytocin superfamily: characterization of a DNA en-
    coding a vasopressin-related precursor, preproconopressin, from the
    mollusc Lymnaea Stagnalis.' *Proc. NY Acad. Sci.* USA 1992; 89:
    4593–7.
6   Leibowitz, M.R. *The chemistry of love.* Little, Brown, Boston, 1983.
7   Marazziti, D., Akiskal, H.S. et al. 'Alteration of the platelet
    serotonin transporter in romantic love.' *Psychol. Med.* 1999; 29; 3:
    741–5.

10   Who's my Mother?

This piece of the broken mirror is not yet well polished. It is obvious that the baby–mother attachment implies, for the baby, the capacity to identify his mother. There have been countless studies exploring foetal and neonatal sensory perceptions. Although such studies provide abundant hard data regarding the maturation of different sensory functions, the comparative roles in baby–mother attachment of the different pieces of information perceived by the foetus and the newborn baby are still speculative.

The Sense of Smell

However, there is considerable evidence that babies rapidly develop their ability to recognise their own mother by her characteristic scent.[1] We must keep in mind that 1–2 per cent of our genes seem to be allocated to the production of smell receptors.[2] There is a tendency to underestimate the importance of the sense of smell among humans, whereas it is well recognised for neonatal adaptation and social behaviour in most mammals.

Today it is well accepted that specialised receptors are sufficiently mature to respond to chemical stimuli during the last months of pregnancy.[3] The plugs blocking the nostrils of the foetus resolve in the middle of intrauterine life, so that odorous substances in the amniotic fluid may come into contact with olfactory receptors in the nose as that fluid is inhaled by the foetus. Odours may also reach these receptors by diffusion from nasal blood vessels. Clear behavioural responses to strong odourants have been reported in babies born more than 2 months before term.[4] Simple experiments have demonstrated that human newborn babies have a special interest for the odour of amniotic fluid during the hour following birth.[5] From this accumulation of facts one can conclude that at birth the odour of the mother is already familiar, and this familiarity undoubt-edly plays a role in the adaptation to extrauterine life.

As early as 1963, Engen demonstrated the sophisticated responses of newborn babies to different odours.[6] It is probable that the sense of smell is one of the best conductors towards the nipple. In 1970, when studying the various environmental conditions needed for an 'early expression of the rooting reflex',[7] I emphasised the importance of creating a favourable olfactory climate in the birthing room, after observing that certain newborn babies cannot find the breast easily if the strong smell characteristic of a hospital environment has not been eliminated. I also learnt from anecdotes that the sense of smell of the mother is particularly acute in the period surrounding birth. A labouring woman can often detect a subtle odour before the midwife or anybody else. It seems obvious that mother and baby use their sense of smell to identify each other immediately after birth.

It is worth mentioning the experiments by MacFarlane demonstrating that a baby younger than 10 days old can distinguish a pad that has been in contact with his mother's breast from a pad that has been in contact with the breast of another mother.[8] A French team of researchers conducted similar experiments, starting from birth.[9] They found that as early as three days after birth, a baby is able to distiguish the odour of its mother's milk from the milk of another mother who gave birth on the same day. Furthermore, the baby can distinguish the odour of the neck of his mother from the odour of her mouth. Hubert Montagner summarised such findings by claiming that a baby is able to establish a chemical identity card of his mother. More recently, Peter Hepper asked mothers to eat garlic or not eat garlic in the last weeks of their pregnancy.[10] After birth, babies of mother who had eaten garlic had a tendency to spend more time than others sniffing garlic-scented pads. Because we mentioned the experiments demonstrating that the odours and pheromones from the armpits play a role in sexual attraction and in the attachment between sexual part-ners, we must also mention a series of five experiments by Cernoch and Porter that were conducted to determine whether newborn babies can recognise their parents through the odours of their armpits alone.[11] Only breastfed babies can recognise their mother's axillary odours from odours produced by other breastfeeding women or non-pregnant women; they cannot recognise the axillary odours of their father.

From physiologists we can learn that during the first hour after birth the levels of noradrenaline (a hormone of the adrenaline family) in the blood of the baby are very high (20–30 fold as compared with later life). This implies that a special zone of the primitive brain (the 'locus coerulus') which has strong connections with the olfactory bulbs is highly activated. This explains how noradrenaline facilitates olfactory learning.

In other words, a great variety of data suggest that recognition through the sense of smell is involved in the mother–baby attachment. I cannot help making one more allusion to the many similarities between mother–baby attachment and the attachment between sexual partners.

Other Sensory Functions

The sense of hearing is also undoubtedly involved in the mother–baby relationship. Before the age of rooming-in, that is to say, when newborn babies used to stay in the nurseries of maternity units, it was well known that many mothers could recognise the voice of their own baby as early as the first day following birth. On the other hand it is certain that babies can recognise the voice of their mother before being born. Anatomical data suggest that the auditory system is mature in the middle of foetal life. One must underline that the foetus can perceive sound vibrations via the ear as a specialised organ, and at the same time can feel via the skin – the most primitive sensory organ – the vibrations of the whole mother's body which accompany the emission of vocal sounds. Foetal hearing has been widely studied for several decades, in particular by Marie Claire Busnel, Carolyn Granier-Defferre and Jean Pierre Lecanuet.[12] It is also worth mentioning a whole group of studies such as the studies by DeCasper and Spence[13] and the studies by Panneton[14] confirming that newborn babies prefer to hear a story their mother had read out loud before birth or a melody she had sung when pregnant.

The results of such studies reinforce the intuitive knowledge that led us, in the 1970s, to organise singing sessions for pregnant women. It seems that the mother's voice is uniquely adapted to reach the foetus and that the baby is adapted to perceive its mother's voice and learn about it before birth. The universality of lullabies is easily interpreted in the age of the scientification of love.

Vision also develops before birth. Although the eyelids remain fused during the first half of intrauterine life, the foetus is aware of light and reacts to lights flashed on the mother's abdomen. At birth vision is well advanced but not yet perfect by adult standards. It is probable that the capacity to distinguish the colours develops gradually during the first 4 months. The newborn baby cannot accommodate its eyes to different distances and seems to be programmed to have a comparatively clear vision of objects that are at a distance of about 1 foot.[15] This suggests the importance of the eye-to-eye contact at the beginning of the mother–baby relationship. It is noticeable that the high level of noradrenaline released by the baby just before birth – which probably facilitates olfactory learning – tends to dilate the pupils, so that, in circumstances when the birth is relatively uninterfered with, the newborn baby has big eyes and large pupils. It is as if the baby was giving a signal to the mother. Finally, even the sense of sight, which may appear as the less primitive – or the most intellectual – of the senses, is probably involved in the mother newborn interaction.

In spite of the current interest in foetal and sensory perceptions, it is still difficult to evaluate their comparative importance for recognition and attachment. The objective of studies in progress is to improve our understanding of the development of the coordination between several sensory functions.

Summary

It seems that the senses of taste, smell and hearing play an important role in the baby's identification of its mother before and after birth.

It is still difficult to evaluate the comparative importance of the different sensory perceptions and their influence on recognition and attachment.

References

1 Winberg, J. and Porter, R.H. 'Olfaction and human neonatal behaviour: clinical implications.' *Acta Paediatr.* 1998; 87: 6–10.

2 Axel, R. 'The molecular logic of smell.' *Sci. Am.* 1995 (Oct): 130–7.

3 Chuah, M.H. and Fardman, A.I. 'Developmental anatomy of the olfactory system.' In Doty, R.L. ed. *Handbook of olfaction and gestation.* Marcel Dekker, New York, 1995: 147–70.

4 Sarnat, H.B. 'Olfactory reflexes in the newborn infant.' *J. Pediatr.* 1978; 92: 624–6.

5 Schaal, B., Marlier, L. and Soussignan, R. 'Responsiveness to the odour of amniotic fluid in the human neonate.' *Biol. Neonate* 1995; 67: 397–406.

6 Engen, T., Lipsitt, L.P. and Kaye, H. 'Olfactory responses and adaptation in the human neonate.' *J. Comp. Physiol. Psychol.* 1963; 56: 73–7.

7 Odent, M. 'The early expression of the rooting reflex.' *Proceedings of the 5th International Congress of Psychosomatic Obstetrics and Gynaecology, Rome 1977.* London: Academic Press, 1977: 1117–19.

8 MacFarlane, J.A. 'Olfaction in the development of social preferences in the human neonate.' In Porter, R. and O'Connor, M. eds *The human neonate in parent–infant interaction.* Ciba Foundation Symposium 33, Amsterdam, Elsevier, 1975: 103–17.

9 Shaal, B. and Hertling, E. 'Synthese des travaux du groupe de Besancon sur l'olfaction.' In Herbinet, E. and Busnel, M.C. eds *L'aube des sens.* Second edition. Paris: Stock, 1991; 361–77.

10 Hepper, P.G. 'Human fetal "olfactory" learning.' *Int. J. Prenatal and Perinatal Psychol. Med.* 1995; 7: 147–51.

11 Cernoch, J.M. and Porter, R.H. 'Recognition of maternal axillary odors by infants.' *Child. Develop.* 1985; 56: 1593–8.

12 Busnel, M.C. and Granier-Deferre, C. 'And what of fetal audition?' In Oliverio, A. and Zappela, M. eds *The behavior of human infants.* New York and London, Plenum Press, 1983: 93–126.

13 DeCasper, A.J. and Spence, M.J. 'Prenatal maternal speech influences newborn's perception of speech sounds.' *Inf. Behav. Dev.*
1986; 9: 133–50.
14 Panneton, R.K. 'Prenatal auditory experience with melodies.' Doc-
toral dissertation, University of North Carolina, Greensboro, 1995.
15 Vurpillot, E. 'Les perceptions visuelles du nourrisson.' In Herbinet,
E. and Busnel, M.C. eds *L'aube des sens.* Stock, Paris, 991: 67–82.

11   Conflicts Between Mother and Foetus

The relations between mother and foetus are the most intimate of human relations. Sensory functions are not the only means of communication. First and foremost there are exchanges that are necessary to life. Directly or indirectly, all the nutritional substances the foetus needs are provided by the maternal blood and the whole foetal waste goes back to the mother.

The concept of a possible conflict is supported by genetic considerations. David Haig, from the museum of comparative zoology at Harvard University, expressed the fruitful theory of genetic conflict in pregnancy.[1, 2] He judiciously stressed that mother and foetus do not carry identical sets of genes: in the child there are both maternally and paternally derived sets of genes. In other words the harmony of interests between mother and foetus is not complete. It is as if, during the evolutionary process, foetal genes are selected to increase the transfer of nutrients, while the maternal genes are selected to set a limit to this transfer.

The Advocate of the Baby

Since the harmony of interests is not complete, one can understand why the baby needs a sort of advocate to express its demands. This is one of the roles played by the placenta, which is to manipulate maternal physiology for foetal benefit. The placenta can send messages to the mother via hormones (such as HCG or Human Placental Lactogen).

An example
An example can demonstrate how deep-rooted the current misunderstanding of this particular function of the placenta is. During pregnancy, one of the bodily messages sent to the mother is to dilute her blood and make it more fluid, so that it

can more easily go where it is urgently needed. The result is an increased blood volume, which can be in the region of 40 per cent. It is therefore understandable that, during pregnancy, measuring the blood concentration of a substance such as haemoglobin (the pigment of the red blood cells) is a way to evaluate the process of blood dilution, and therefore to test the activity of the placenta. It is easy to anticipate that this concentration, which is usually around 12 to 13 (g/dl), will dramatically decrease during pregnancy.

The objective of one large-scale study by a London team was to explore the relation between maternal haemoglobin concentration and birth outcomes.[3] Birth outcomes of 153,602 pregnancies were analysed. They found that the highest average birth weight was in the group of women who had a haemoglobin concentration of between 8.5 and 9.5. Their main conclusion was that the magnitude of the fall in haemogloblin concentration is related to birth weight. A similar pattern occurred in all ethnic groups. Furthermore it appeared that when the haemoglobin concentration fails to fall below 10.5, there is an increased risk of low birth weight and preterm delivery. Similar conclusions have been reached by other – yet smaller – epidemiological studies.[4, 5]

Although such studies were published in authoritative medical journals with an international readership, all over the world millions of pregnant women are wrongly told that they are anaemic and are given iron supplements. Such a diagnosis is not often based on the results of the specific tests that evaluate the iron status and detect an authentic anaemia. The inability to interpret such a simple test as haemoglobin concentrations in pregnancy is intriguing because it is quasi-universal. It is widespread … beyond belief.

A Japanese lady spent the first half of her pregnancy in London, before going back to Tokyo. One of her European friends – who had four babies – warned her long in advance that at the end of her pregnancy she will be told that she is anaemic and given iron tablets. You can guess the end of the story, which happened on the other side of the world. Furthermore, the inability to interpret the test is widespread, whatever the medical circle one considers. In a prestigious medical journal an authoritative team of British epidemiologists published a study of the third stage of labour, that is between the birth of the baby and the delivery of the placenta.[6] In order to concentrate on low-risk pregnancies they eliminated all women whose haemoglobin was below 10. The team concluded that the average concentration in the population they studied was 11.1. I was subsequently given an opportunity to indicate some of the limitations of this study.[7]

Such a global phenomenon is worrying for those who understand that one of the main roles of health professionals should be to protect the emotional state of pregnant women. More precisely it should be to avoid the 'nocebo effect' of prenatal consultations. There is a nocebo effect whenever health professionals do more harm than good by interfering with the beliefs, the imagination, and therefore the emotional state of a person. So when a healthy, pregnant woman is told that she needs iron tablets in order to correct an imbalance in her bodily functions, there is a nocebo effect.

A lack of interest in placental physiology is at the root of such misinterpretations. Many practitioners, instead of being obsessed by the risk of anaemia, would do better to look at conflicting situations revealed by too high haemoglobin concentrations. Few practitioners can visualise the spectacular dilution of the blood of pregnant women. That is why many of them do not pay attention to studies that would turn their preconceptions upside down.

The lack of interest in placental physiology is deeply rooted. The French psychoanalyst Bernard This understands the many implications of the common tendency to forget the placenta. He studied what he calls the 'myth of the fusion' between mother and foetus.[8] The myth of the fusion is incompatible with the concept of conflict in pregnancy. The tendency to forget the placenta is connected with the socialisation of birth and all the beliefs and rituals that interfere with the physiological processes. When, at the cultural level, women do not give birth but are 'delivered' by a person who rushes to cut the cord, the placenta is forgotten.

Other examples
The placenta can also tell the mother about an increased need for sugar: this leads to a modification of the metabolism of

carbohydrates. In exceptional cases the effect will be a real disease, when the demand by the placenta is too high and the mother's body cannot control the situation.

In most cases the response of the maternal body remains in the framework of physiology. Unfortunately many practitioners do not then hesitate to use the term 'gestational diabetes', without realising its powerful nocebo effect. When a woman is given this diagnosis she tends to confuse what is a transitory response to foetal needs with a serious chronic disease. Such a term can transform overnight a happy pregnant woman into a sick person. Professor John Jarrett, from London, claims that gestational diabetes is a 'nonentity'.[9] In a letter to the *American Journal of Obstetrics and Gynecology* it has been called 'a diagnosis still looking for a disease'. Today there is a debate on whether pregnant women should be screened for glucose tolerance. A large-scale study on the entire Canadian population revealed that the routine use of the tests to detect gestational diabetes did not improve the outcomes.[10] This diagnosis is useless because, when it has been established, it leads to simple recommendations that should be given to all pregnant women, such as: avoid pure sugar (soft drinks, etc.), include complex carbohydrates (pasta, bread, rice, etc.) in your diet and take sufficient and regular physical exercise.

Once more there is a discrepancy between scientific studies and daily practice. Once more, at the root of this discrepancy there is a lack of interest in the functions of the placenta. The placenta can also demand of the mother that she increase her blood pressure because mother and foetus need more blood. In most cases the increased blood pressure can be considered a physiological response. It is not associated with any metabolic imbalance. It is 'gestational hypertension'. Several epidemiological studies clearly demonstrate that such an increased blood pressure is associated with positive outcomes.[11,12,13,14] Unfortunately it will often be presented as bad news. Many practitioners tend to confuse the issue of 'gestational hypertension' with that of pre-eclampsia, which is an uncontrolled conflict.

Pre-eclampsia

With pre-eclampsia we are undoubtedly in the field of pathology. Let us recall that pre-eclampsia is a disease of late pregnancy (usually first pregnancy). It is life-threatening for baby and for mother. Early detection of this disease was originally the main reason for introducing the concept of prenatal care during the twentieth century. According to the most common definitions, pre-eclampsia implies the association of high blood pressure and the presence of a certain amount of protein in the urine in a 24-hour period. There are usually other detectable metabolic imbalances. When there are seizures the disease is called eclampsia. The old term toxaemia – which included pre-eclampsia and eclampsia – is now out of fashion.

Interspecies comparisons can help in understanding human pre-eclampsia. Veterinarians use the word eclampsia to refer to a life-threatening disease that can occur in other mammals such as dogs. The typical story is that of a bitch whose litters are large. At the end of her pregnancy or at the beginning of lactation the bitch will be restless and nervous. Within a short time she will walk with a stiff gait and may even wobble or appear disoriented. Eventually she may be unable to walk and exhibit extreme leg rigidity. Death can occur if no treatment is given. For the veterinarians there is no doubt that this disease is the consequence of a conflict between bitch and pups. The bodies of some bitches simply cannot keep up with the increased demands in nutrients, particularly calcium. In other words there is a conflict between the demands expressed by the foetuses and what the mother can supply without depleting her own body. This interpretation is confirmed by the spectacular effect of an intravenous calcium supplementation.

One must emphasise that where dogs are concerned the priority at the end of pregnancy and the beginning of lactation is to feed the bones of the pups, which are much more mature at birth than those of human babies. It is therefore not surprising that in this species the so-called eclampsia is in fact mostly related to low calcium levels.

If there is a possible conflict in mammals between genes expressed in the mother and genes expressed in the foetus/placenta, this leads to inevitable questions regarding the most probable reasons for a mother–offspring conflict in the human species. Among humans the priority is not to have strong bones at birth. The priority is to feed the developing brain. The spectacular growth spurt of the brain during the second half of foetal life is a specifically human trait. Let us recall that the size of the human brain at birth is one-quarter of the adult size, whereas the size of the entire body is only one-twentieth of the adult size. One can conclude that in our species, when there is a conflict between the demands expressed by the foetus and what the mother can do without depleting her body, we should look first at the huge needs of the developing brain.

Today the specific needs of the developing brain are well understood.[15] Fat comprises 60 per cent of the brain. This means that the main nutritional needs are in terms of fatty acids. Details of complex biochemical processes can be found in other sources,[16] but, put simply, the developing brain has special needs in terms of long chain polyunsaturated fatty acids, particularly those of the omega 3 family. It is worth mentioning that the long chain fatty acids of the omega 3 family are abundant and preformed in the seafood chain. These mere facts can help in understanding the basis of a new theory of pre-eclampsia.

One can present pre-eclampsia as the price certain humans have to pay for having a large brain, and the cost is that nutritional needs are not perfectly met. It is much easier to meet the enormous needs of the developing brain when the diet includes seafood. It appears that pregnant women[17] (and probably *Homo sapiens* in general) ideally need a certain balance between food from the land and food from the sea. Finally one can propose that pre-eclampsia is the price some human beings must pay for having a large brain while they are more or less separated from the seafood chain. The expression of maternal foetal conflicts offers new perspectives from which to study human nature.[18]

All the disciplines relevant to the 'Scientification of Love' underline the importance of the very first contact between mother and newborn baby. The meaning of this first contact becomes clearer after referring to different situations of mother–foetus conflict.

Summary

A reference to the conflicts between mother and foetus offers a new perspective from which to interpret the short period following birth, which is critical in the development of the mother–child attachment.

References

1 Haig, D. 'Genetic conflicts in human pregnancy.' *Quarterly Review of Biology* 1993; 68 (4); 495–531.

2 Haig, D. 'Altercations of generations: genetic conflicts of pregnancy.' *Am. J. Reprod. Immunol.* 1996; 35 (3): 226–36.

3 Steer, P., Alam, M.A., Wadsworth, J. and Welch, A. 'Relation between maternal haemoglobin concentration and birth weight in different ethnic groups.' *BMJ* 1995; 310: 489–91.

4 Koller, O., Sandvei, R. and Sagen, N. 'High hemoglobin levels during pregnancy and fetal risk.' *Int. J. Gynaecol. Obstet.* 1980; 18: 53–6.

5 Garn, S.M. et al. 'Maternal hematologic levels and pregnancy outcome.' *Semin. Perinatol.* 1981; 5: 155–62.

6 Rogers, J., Wood, J., et al. 'Active versus expectant management of third stage of labour: the Hinchingbrooke randomised controlled trial.' *Lancet* 1998; 351: 693–9.

7 Odent, M. 'Active versus expectant management of third stage of labour.' *Lancet* 1998; 351: 1659.

8 This, B. 'Le sacrifice du placenta.' In Bernard This, *Naitre … et sourire.* Paris: Aubier Montaigne 1977; 182–208.

9 Jarrett, R.J. 'Gestational diabetes: a non-entity?' *BMJ* 1993; 306: 37–8.

10 Wen, S.W., Liu, S., Kramer, M.S., et al. 'Impact of prenatal glucose screening on the diagnosis of gestational diabetes and on pregnancy outcomes.' *Am. J. Epidemiol.* 2000; 152 (11): 1009–14.

11 Symonds, E.M. 'Aetiology of pre-eclampsia: a review.' *J. R. Soc. Med.* 1980; 73: 871–5.

12 Naeye, E.M. 'Maternal blood pressure and fetal growth.' *Am. J. Obstet. Gynecol.* 1981; 141: 780–7.

13 Kilpatrick, S. 'Unlike pre-eclampsia, gestational hypertension is not associated with increased neonatal and maternal morbidity except abruptio.' SPO abstracts. *Am. J. Obstet. Gynecol.* 1995; 419: 376.
14 Curtis, S., et al. 'Pregnancy effects of non-proteinuric gestational hypertension.' SPO Abstracts. *Am. J. Obst. Gynecol.* 1995; 418: 376.
15 Crawford, M.A., Hassam, A.C., Williams, G. and Whitehouse, W.L. 'Essential fatty acids and fetal brain growth.' *Lancet* 1976; I: 452–3.
16 Odent, M. 'Pre-eclampsia as a maternal fetal conflict.' ISSFAL (International Society for the Study of Fatty Acids and Lipids) *News.* 2000; 7 (3): 7–10.
17 Odent, M., McMillan, L. and Kimmel, T. 'Prenatal care and sea fish.' *Eur. J. Obstet. Gynecol.* 1996; 68 (1,2): 49–51.
18 Odent, M. 'The primary human disease. An evolutionary perspective.' *ReVision* 1995; 18 (2): 19–21.

12   Love of Animals for Humans

It is significant that the scientification of love started with a story of animal attachment for human beings. Konrad Lorenz did not hesitate to use the word 'love' when referring to the ducks and geese who remained attached during their whole life to the first large body they met after being born.

At the Root of our Civilisations

The importance of Lorenz' observations is more than historical. The relationship between certain species of animals and humans is at the very root of our civilisations. The domestication of animals has been a determinant step in the history of mankind. It is a major aspect of our domination of nature, that is to say of our strategy for survival.

From the time when domesticated animals were used not only to obtain meat and skin, but also for cooperating with humans, a certain degree of affective attachment between animals and humans became an advantage, and even a necessity. This represents a recent phase of our relationship with the animal kingdom. It is probably less than 10,000 years ago that dogs started to accompany hunters and helped them hunt wild animals; they probably also guarded human settlements and warned the inhabitants of possible danger. It was during the second millennium BC that peoples inhabiting the Middle East started to use horses in chariot battles. Early domestication of the cat was probably the result of the pleasure experienced from keeping this animal. The cat's ability to catch mice and rats was surely another reason that impelled people to keep cats at home. In Ancient Egypt the cat was considered a sacred animal. Cows, at the initial stages of domestication, produced a small amount of milk, sufficient only to rear their calves. The development of high milk yield and the breeding of cows especially for milk production is a later event in the history of domestication.

An Aspect of the Scientification of Love

One can wonder how mammals whose ancestors were wild and had no interest for our species developed their capacity to be attached to us. Clear answers to such questions are offered through a recent and little known aspect of the scientification of love. For example Sato[1] in Japan, and Boissy and Bouissou[2] in France, made experiments to determine what would make heifers tractable: they demonstrated the positive effects of early handling. Boivin,[3] in France, found that the weaning artificially induced by man is not enough to tame goat kids: kids need to be previously handled by human beings in order to seek human contact later on in life. According to several researchers, such as Mal[4] and Larose,[5] halter training in foals is facilitated by early human handling.

Whatever the species of mammals scientists are studying, they always underline the paramount importance of early sensitive periods in the development of animal–human attachment. We must notice that humans usually express a strong interest in the offspring of their domesticated animals. When I was at a primary school in a French village, the children of farmers were exceptionally talkative when describing newborn piglets, as if they were aware of the significance of their first encounter with them.

The importance of early sensitive periods is consciously recognised regarding mammals who have not been used as pets for a long time. This is the case of the Tamworth pigs, who were prized in the past for their rich and aromatic bacon. Today these pigs may be kept as pets, but only if they are tamed from birth. Even Bengal tigers can cooperate with human beings in circuses, but only if they were born in captivity, and therefore in contact with members of our species at a very early age.

The Price Paid for Domestication

Domesticated animals have few opportunities to take the initiative, to struggle for life and to compete. The side effects can be evaluated in terms of the evolution of the species. In a great variety of mammals such as pigs, sheep, dogs, cats, camels, ferrets and mink, one of the long-term effects of domestication is a significant reduction in brain size.[6] The changes in the brain of a wild creature into that of a highly domesticated strain happen very rapidly in terms of evolution – after only 120 years and generations of domestication, a brain size reduction of about 20 per cent has been observed in mink.[7] And what about Homo? Neanderthal man had a larger brain than ours ...

Summary

Since the domestication of animals represents a determinant step in the history of humankind, the development of animal–human attachment is a relevant aspect of the 'scientification of love'.

References

1 Sato, et al. 'The effects of early caressing on later tractability of calves.' *Japan. J Zootech. Sci.* 1984; 55: 332–8.
2 Boissy, P. and Bouissou, M.F. 'Effects of early handling on heifers subsequent reactivity to humans and to unfamiliar situations.' *Appl. Anim. Behav. Sci.* 1988; 20: 259–73.
3 Boivin, X. and Braastad, B.O. 'Effects of handling during temporary isolation after early weaning on goat kids' later response to humans.' *Appl. Anim. Behav. Sci.* 1996; 48: 61–71.
4 Mal, M.E. and McCall, C.A. 'The influence of handling during different ages in a halter training test in foals.' *Appl. Anim. Behav. Sci.* 1996; 50:115–20.
5 Larose, C. 'Étude de l'impact de manipulations sur le comportement du poulain.' Thèse, 1997, Université de Rennes, CNRS 6552

6 Kruska, D. 'Mammalian domestication and its effect on the brain structure and behavior.' In Jerison, I. ed. *Intelligence and evolutionary biology*. Springer, Berlin, Heidelberg, 1988: 211–50.
7 Kruska, D. 'The effect of domestication on brain size and composition in the mink.' *J. Zool. London* 1996; 239: 645–61.

13   Orgasmic States, Ecstatic States and Mystical Emotions

It is surprising that the orgasms of genital sexuality have rarely been considered in the context of changed levels of consciousness – they are, after all, common experiences and are shared by males and females alike. They are better understood when a parallel is drawn with other changed levels of consciousness. I have heard at least a dozen women who spontaneously used the word 'orgasm' to refer to the birth of their baby. The interest of such comparisons is renewed at a time when it is possible to 'map the brain', even during orgasm. Thanks to new imaging techniques, Finnish researchers clearly demonstrated that during an orgasm the neocortex is at rest, apart from the 'right prefrontal cortex'.[1] It is easy to understand why the sort of orgasmic states that can accompany the last contractions of the 'foetus ejection reflex' have been ignored. Most cultures have denied the need for privacy in the period around birth and have tended to socialise this event and to disturb it with their beliefs and associated rituals.

Orgasm as a State of Consciousness

A key to a better understanding of these orgasmic states is to take into account the similarities with other ecstatic states: 'Moments of ecstasy have recurred like grace notes throughout my life.... The ecstasy of sexual union is akin to that of ecstatic prayer. Both involve a loss of self-consciousness ....'[2] Una Kroll is one of those who elegantly highlighted the similarities between the emotions of sexual union and mystical emotions. A young mother told me that, immediately after giving birth, she saw the whole universe in her baby's eyes.

It is not new to regard orgasmic states as a way to reach a cosmic consciousness. Old Tantric texts that remained unknown in the West until quite recently teach sexual rituals practised by the Hindu Cult of Ecstasy in order to attain the cosmic Oneness. This is what is commonly called Tantric sex. A parable found in a Tantric text, written in Sanskrit 2,000 years ago, is highly significant.[3] It is the story of a hermit pilgrim in search of 'The Supreme Truth'. He had been travelling, meditating, fasting, inflicting unbearable pain upon himself for many years, but he could never reach the Supreme Truth. One day, disillusioned by years of unrewarded effort, he rested in the late afternoon by a river. A female Tantric Master came by, to bathe and anoint her body. After listening to the pilgrim's story she seduced him by 'carrying his senses through Tantric pleasures to the state of extremest arousal, wherein he found the centre of power he sought, awaiting him in what he had so long denied himself'. More recently even Freud – who was not considered a mystic – accepted that there is one sort of circumstance when the limits of the ego can disappear and that is during a sexual climax.

All these links are acceptable and plausible in the scientific context of the late 1990s. From a physiological point of view, it can even seem quite difficult to interpret mystical experiences without referring to orgasmic states. We might say that orgasmic states and mystical emotions are two pieces of the broken mirror that are easy to connect.

It helps to recall the double meaning of the word 'mystical'. The Greek word simultaneously suggests 'closing the senses', i.e. eliminating a certain sort of knowledge, and entering the 'mysteries', i.e. having access to another sort of knowledge.

The Old and the New

Today the nature of orgasmic states and other ecstatic states can be seen in terms of the relationship between the human neocortical supercomputer, and older, more archaic structures which we share with all other mammals. Our new brain supports the concepts of time, space and boundaries, including the limits of our life-span. These concepts define our sense of identity, which only develops in infancy once the human neocortex is sufficiently developed, and seems to correspond to that stage when the child is able to recognise herself in a mirror. When we are wide awake we see the universe from a neocortical perspective.

The older sub-neocortical structures, on the other hand, provide us with our sense of being part of a whole. They support another reality – one that transcends the concepts of space and time and boundaries. These archaic brain structures cannot be dissociated from our basic adaptive systems – the hormonal and immune systems (in the wider context of the 'primal adaptive system'), and our emotions and instincts are engendered by their activity.[4] We might look upon the neocortex originally as a useful tool which served the old structures as a means of supporting our survival instinct.

The Need to Escape

In the age of the scientification of love one cannot avoid questions about the function of such changes of consciousness as ecstatic states in general and orgasmic states in particular. Today it is well accepted that, when fighting is impossible, there is only one way to protect our health in adverse circumstances and that is to escape. There are many ways to escape and to refuse to submit to a situation – going into a reality other than space and time reality is just one of them.

This new vision of the functions of orgasmic and ecstatic states leads us to recall one of the most important advances in our understanding of health and disease in the past few decades. It has been identifying the prototype of pathogenic (disease creating) situations – being trapped in adverse or threatening circumstances and being unable to either fight or flee. When we can only passively submit, our health tends to deteriorate.[5] On the other hand, being in a position to take the initiative is health enhancing.

The story began with simple experiments with cats and dogs who became sick after receiving a series of electric shocks.[6, 7] It was not the electric shocks in themselves that made the animals ill, but the submissive state they were in at the time they received the shocks. Their health was not endangered when they had the opportunity to fight a companion (another animal in the cage), or if they had some means of escape, even though all the groups studied finally received the same number of electric shocks. There is an altered hormonal balance during 'uncontrollable adverse events' which suggests that when we have lost all hope and given up, a self-destructive process starts. Much of the data published in the medical literature confirms that the results of such experiments with rats and dogs can be transposed to human subjects. Among humans situations of 'learned helplessness', 'learned hopelessness' and 'inhibition of action' have been widely explored. The health effects of certain extreme situations of 'inhibition of action' are well documented, such as the life-long diseases of prisoners who have been tortured, or the health problems of children repeatedly bullied at school.[8]

In the current scientific context, the dangers of an excess of domestication in human beings are easily interpreted. Civilised human beings have countless opportunities to feel trapped by circumstances, that is to say many reasons to try to escape from the daily realities of life. This may explain the cross-cultural need for transcendence. This universal human need has many similarities with sexual desire. It is striking that human societies have always been inclined to control and channel both sexual desire and the need for transcendence.

Summary

Orgasmic states, and other ecstatic states, may be regarded as ways of refusing to submit to a situation, by escaping into another, out-of-space-and-time reality. It is well accepted that, when fighting is impossible as a self-defence strategy, there is only one way to protect our health in adverse circumstances and that is to escape.

References

1 Tiihonen, J. et al. 'Increase in cerebral blood flow of right prefrontal cortex in man during orgasm.' *Neurosci. Lett.* 1994; 170; 2: 241–3.
2 Kroll, Una. 'A womb-centred life.' In Hurcombe, Linda ed. *Sex and God*. Routledge and Kegan Paul,. London, 1987: 102.
3 Thirleby, Ashley. *Tantra: the key to sexual power and pleasure*. Jaico, Bombay, 1982.
4 Odent, M. *Primal health*. Century Hutchinson, London, 1986.
5 Maier, S.F. and Seligman, M.E.P. 'Learned helplessness: theory and evidence.' *J. Exp. Psychol. General* 1976; 105: 3–46.
6 Laborit, H. *L'inhibition de l'action*. Masson, Paris, 1980.
7 Seligman, M.E.P. and Beagley, C. 'Learned helplessness in the rat.' *J. Comp. Physiol. Psychol.* 1975; 88: 534–41.
8 Williams, K., Chambers, M., Logan, S. and Robinson, D. 'Association of common health symptoms with bullying in primary school children.' *BMJ* 1996; 313: 17–19.

14   Love of the Whole

When considering how different episodes of our sexual life can culminate in an orgasmic climax, we realised that we were focusing on one link in a long chain of the various levels of consciousness. We highlighted the ill-defined limits between orgasmic states, ecstatic states and mystical emotions.

Mystical emotions have been interpreted as 'love of the whole'. It is therefore relevant to include in the scientific studies of love references to the emotional states that can be deemed to be mystical. The 'oceanic feeling' we might experience on a beach at sunset is one example of this type of emotional state.

Beyond the Scope of Physiological Explorations

Mystical emotions are more likely to occur in certain situations such as darkness, solitude, silence.... Artistic activities – those artifices employed by humans to harmonise their two brains – can induce mystical emotions. In any artistic activity a technique – made possible by the specifically human neocortex – is serving a function which, in turn, is controlled by the older structures. The technique of a musician makes it possible to transmit emotions through sound. The technique of a painter can transmit emotions via visual signals. Poetry is another way of expressing emotions by means of one elaborated form of communication called 'language'. The technique of a dancer tends to arouse emotions induced by body movements and rhythms. Gastronomy is related to digestive functions; the art of the perfumier to our sense of smell; eroticism to the mating instinct.

There is no physiological function that cannot be the basis of some artistic activity, and all forms of artistic activity have the power to induce subtle or intense emotions that can be experienced as mystical. Singing, by very definition, offers a particularly apt example of the harmonisation between the two brains – melody and rhythm are associated with the use of words to communicate emotions. Furthermore, certain works of art – Gothic cathedrals, Indian temples, the Egyptian Sphinx, Sanskrit hymns, Bach music, Gregorian plainsong, for example – came into being originally by very reason of man's need to convey mystical emotions.

There is an infinite range of mystical emotions in terms of purity and intensity, from the discreet mystical nuance as an integral part of some complex emotional states, to the pure and intense 'peak experience'. Since the 'peak experience' has been reported in a great number of cultures, there are many other ways of describing it – 'cosmic experience', 'mystical union', 'enlightenment', 'nirvana', 'mystical ecstasy' and so on.

By analysing 43 cases of 'cosmic consciousness' at the beginning of this century, Richard Buke was able to identify some marked characteristics of this particular state.[1] More recent descriptions by psychologists such as Arthur Deikman confirm Buke's conclusions.[2] First the experience is a paroxysm, a climax, a culmination, and there is invariably a speedy return to normality. The 'peak experience' is characterised by a consciousness of the Oneness of everything – 'All in One and One in All' – and also, by the sense of timelessness, which implies a sense of immortality. 'Peak experiences' have a quality of passivity – the mystic feels as if his or her own will were in abeyance, and the person is held by a power not his own, and it is interesting that this passivity is associated with a feeling of infinite peace and infinite love of everything in creation – a sense of infinite well-being. A subjective light, or the concept of illumination are almost always mentioned. In retrospect the experience is associated with a conviction of absolute 'realness'.

In fact, there is a problem of communication in these reports because many mystics have been reluctant to relate these experiences that seem to defy any verbal description. This is illustrated by a comment made by Thomas Aquinas, author of *Summa Theologica*, after a cosmic experience: 'I have seen that which makes all that I have written and taught look insignificant to me. My writing days are over.' In contrast, the mystic's entourage sometimes offer more descriptive information. These close observers note the transformation of a person who has had a real cosmic experience, often using adjectives like 'more charming', 'more attractive' and even 'charismatic'.

While a 'peak experience' can be a one-off for some people, it can be repeated in the life of others. In cases when it becomes a frequent occurrence it has been called 'the illuminative life'.

What Physiologists can Explore

The pure, authentic, 'peak experience' is rare, and typically occurs in unpredictable circumstances. That is why it cannot be explored scientifically. Artificially induced states of conscious-ness cannot reach the absolute purity and intensity of an authentic 'peak experience', but some can be studied with scientific methods.

According to Ingrid Mueller from Munich, there is a specific hormonal profile during an ecstatic shamanic trance, quite different from that found in any other altered state, including a hypnotic trance.[3] Levels of cortisol, adrenaline and noradrena-line rise briefly, then drop dramatically, whereas the level of endorphins is increasing. The combination of low blood pres-sure and an increased pulse rate may explain why shamans say that they die during a trance. Furthermore there are very slow brain waves of six or seven cycles per second.

The states of consciousness induced by psychedelic drugs are comparatively easy to study with scientific methods. Numerous psychedelic substances have been used down through the ages, from the milky exudate obtained from the unripe seed pods of the poppy (opium) and the 'sacred' mushroom of Mexico, up to the modern, synthetic LSD. The physiological effects of LSD have been well documented, and, in particular, its stimulating effects on the autonomous nervous system. Stan Grof's work on the effects of LSD[4] made a huge contribution to the develop-ment of a new discipline known as 'transpersonal psychology' which, in fact, was what originally sparked my interest in what I would call the 'mystical emotions'. One of the main reactions to the use of LSD is an altered perception of space and time, as in any mystical emotion.

The effects of fasting on the relationship between neocortical and subcortical activities have not yet been seriously explored scientifically, but it is well understood that fasting tends to decrease the level of blood glucose, the main fuel of the neocortex. Furthermore, fasting induces deficiencies – in zinc, for example – that, in turn, alter brain activity. This is well known by psychiatrists who use zinc in therapy.

The levels of consciousness reached in Zen and yoga meditation have been explored with electroencephalography (EEG). It seems that any deep state of relaxation and well-being is characterised by alpha brain waves. These alpha rhythms in the occipital cortex in particular are associated with decreased visual attention to the external environment. In a study of the EEG trances of Zen practitioners of the Soto and Rinzai sects, alpha waves were observed within 50 seconds. As the trace continued these alpha waves were joined by a rhythmical theta trace which is observable in a hypnotic state. The traces exactly reflected the disciples' mental states evaluated by a Zen master.[5]

I attach great importance to a study by Elmer Green who found that the Swami Rama can reach a delta rhythm without falling asleep although a delta brain wave is supposed to characterise deep sleep.[6] These findings tend to support the theory that deep sleep is associated with the cosmic, out-of-space-and-time reality. It seems that, when we are wide awake and we rely on our neocortical computer in a space-and-time reality, we remain imprinted with 'the other reality'. This may explain the motivation behind the impulse to do extraordinary things, such as build cathedrals. The EEG studies tend to confirm that a reduction in the activity of the neocortex is a prerequisite to reach an out-of-space-and-time reality, and a sense of Oneness.

Interestingly enough, the EEG rhythm of non-human mammals such as rats is the equivalent of a delta rhythm. Is cosmic consciousness a phylogenetically old state of consciousness, i.e. archaic in the context of the evolutionary process? This appears to be borne out if we consider the development of an individual human being. Since the pioneering work of Margaret Mahler it has been well accepted that the human newborn baby – whose neocortex is at an early stage of its development – does not yet have any sense of self, and countless developmental psychologists have explored how 'oneness' becomes 'our own separate self'.[7] The title of a book by Louise Kaplan is highly significant: Oneness and separateness: from infant to individual.[8]

This opposition between the archaic brain structures and the recent neocortical structures needs to be emphasised at a time when the general public is hearing so much about another duality – between the 'left brain' and the 'right brain'. We know that the brain hemispheres have a tendency to specialise and to complement each other. Today it is common knowledge that the left, verbal hemisphere tends to operate in a logical, analytical fashion while the right hemisphere is more specialised in non-analytical global perception. Every day we learn a little more about brain asymmetry thanks to new techniques such as Positron Emission Tomography (PET) and functional magnetic resonance imaging. For example, a Canadian study of more than 1,000 musicians found that their 'planum temporal' is highly developed in the left side of the brain. Of course, there are good reasons to have a simple vision of the right hemisphere as being more 'intuitive' than the left, and apparently more directly in touch with the primitive brain. However, where the need for transcendence, the sexual instinct, and the drive for survival are concerned, the actual duality is between the older, deeper structures and the newer ones. Only humans have developed such sophisticated associative areas – such an elaborated neocortical supercomputer.

Certain brain structures can act as intermediaries between the most archaic structures and the most recent neocortical zones. A conjunction of perspectives suggests that this is the case in brain structures we share with all the mammals (the limbic system includes deep temporal lobes and associated old structures). It has been well known for a long time that feelings of religious ecstasy can be linked with right temporal epilepsy.[9] Mystical experiences have been induced by stimulating the right temporal lobe with a weak electric current.[10] Let us add that the drug ketamine, that acts in the limbic system, can induce an altered perception of space and time.[11]

The Ability to Build Bridges

It seems that there are major differences between one individual and another regarding their capacity to build bridges between the different realities. It seems that some people have developed their own means of escape because they are in poor health and probably cannot rely on a strong orgasmic potential, and so acquired a reputation for being 'holy' or mystical. Thomas Aquinas was stricken by illness and died at the age of 50, two months after being personally summoned by Pope Gregory X – a highly pathogenic situation. One of the most striking common points between the best-known women mystics of medieval Europe was their poor health.[12] Hildegard of Bingen, scientist, visionary, poet and theologian, suffered from illness of a migraine-type for most of her life, often being unable to move for days at a time. In her first great visionary book *Scivias* she explained how she was 'troubled by continual pain in all her veins, marrow and flesh...', and she also noted that it was through this disabling experience that she could perceive 'some of the mysteries of God'. Clare of Assisi, the close friend of Saint Francis and founder of the community of Poor Clares, was bedridden for most of her adult life. Mechtild of Magdeburg, the poet of the Beguine Movement of women's communities, wrote that, for 20 years, she was 'never but tired, ill and weak'. The visions of Julian of Norwich began in an illness in which she hung between life and death. As for Catherine of Siena, whose major writing consists of a dialogue between herself and God, she died at 33, being unable to eat.

Some centuries later, Saint Bernadette of Lourdes, who spent a great part of her life in prayer, died at the age of 35 from a disease identified by some as bone cancer, or disseminated tuberculosis by others.

After interpreting the healing function of ecstatic states and mystical emotions it is also worth trying to interpret the need to escape by means of alcohol or the use of hallucinogenic drugs. The need to escape by artificial means may indicate a failure of the physiological mechanisms that change our consciousness.

Western medicine must adapt to new concepts and realise that the function of multiple realities has become a serious topic for investigation and reflection.

A Great Diversity of Roads

It is commonplace to stress that there is an infinite diversity of roads leading to cosmic consciousness. Physiologists are able to interpret this diversity. When subcortical structures are not repressed by cortical activity they can release high levels of hormones such as opiates in a great many different circumstances. For example, extreme pain and extreme pleasure are associated with high levels of endorphins, and any intense emotion implies a reduction of neocortical control. Soldiers and rapists may have an orgasm at the moment of killing. Among so many life events, we now have good reason to include certain cases of 'near death experience'. Some people who have been resuscitated and survived, having appeared to be dead with EEG traces that were flat, use words to describe what it was like that are very similar to the language used to describe a mystical 'peak' experience. Also, the 'near death experience' tends to transform the personality and change the life of its survivors. Brain death occurs in phases. When the neocortex stops functioning there is probably a transitory phase of unrepressed activity of the primitive brain and a flood of hormones, including opiates. In other words, the dying of the neocortex might be another way to reach a peak mystical experience and to enter an out-of-space-and-time reality. Criminals being executed have been observed to ejaculate. Orgasm, death and peak experience are three closely related topics.

Summary

The sort of emotional states that can be deemed 'mystical' should be included in scientific studies of love, if they are interpreted as 'love of the whole'. Evidence from a number of perspectives suggests that the old brain structures which we share with all mammals play a central role in mystical emotions.

References

1 Buke, R.M. *Cosmic consciousness*. Dutton, New York, 1969: Part 3, 61–82.
2 Deikmann, A.J. 'Deautomatization and the mystic experience.' *Psychiatry 1966; 29: 324–38.*
3 Gore, Belinda *Ecstatic body postures*. Bear and Co., Santa Fe, 1995.
4 Grof, S. *Realms of the human unconscious: observations from LSD research*. Viking Press, New York, 1975.
5 Tart, C. ed. *Altered states of consciousness*. Wiley, NewYork, 1969.
6 Green, E.E., Green, A.M. and Laters, W. 'Voluntary control of internal states: psychological and physiological.' *Journal of Transpersonal Psychology* 1970; 2; 1.
7 Mahler, Margaret, Pine, Fred and Berman, Anne *One human symbiosis and the vicissitudes of individuation, vol. II: the psychological birth of the human infant*. Basic Books, New York, 1967.
8 Kaplan, Louise J. *Oneness to separateness: from infant to individual*. Touchton Books (Simon and Schuster), 1978.
9 Williams, D. 'The structure of emotions reflecting in epileptic experiences.' Brain 1956; 79: 29–67.
10 Persinger, M. *The neuropsychological bases of good beliefs*. Praeger, New York, 1987.
11 Morse, M.L., Venecia, D. and Milstein, J. 'Near-death experiences: a neurophysiological explanatory model.' *J. Near Death Studies* 1989; 1: 45–53.
12 Furlong, Monica *Visions and longings*. Mowbray, London, 1960.

15   Links between Birthing and Praying

A Way to Explore Human Nature

My interest in prayer as a way to explore human nature began in unusual circumstances. I was thinking about the most common positions used by women in spontaneous labour, when they do not feel observed or guided, and when they do not have a preconceived idea of how birth should be. More often than not, they are in some sort of bending-forward posture. During labour, it is quite common for them to be on their hands and knees. During the very last expulsive contractions when there is a tendency to be more upright, many women remain on their knees although others may stand up and lean over the edge of a piece of furniture, but still bending forward. When I look back at my experience of home births I realise that, in a majority of cases, I must get behind the woman to see the baby coming.

This typical behaviour makes sense from the point of view of anyone trying to understand the birth process. Obviously many women are attracted to being on all fours as a way of dealing with their pain, especially back pain. Not only do certain postures help to reduce the mother's pain, they can also facilitate the necessary rotation of the baby's body inside the pelvis. Again, when she is bending forward, it ensures that her major blood vessels – the vena cava and the aorta – are not being compressed between the weight of the baby in the uterus and the mother's spine, which otherwise would tend to impede the blood flow to and from the placenta. In short, the chances of foetal distress during labour are minimised when the mother bends forward. These mechanical advantages are easy to explain so we tend to miss the most important point, which is that when a labouring woman is on all fours she isolates herself from the outside world more easily. She is in the best possible position to reduce the activity of her neocortex and therefore to stimulate the release of the hormones which promote effective uterine contractions. This vision of a mother 'going to another planet', on her hands and knees, is highly suggestive of the connection between birthing and praying.

If praying is ubiquitous, it is probably because it corresponds to a biological need. This is as pervasive as the need for transcendence. Like singing and laughing, praying is specifically human behaviour. Any study of *homo sapiens* should involve questioning the physiology and function of prayer. Praying effectively reduces the activity of the neocortical super-computer, and may help some people to reach another reality, out-of-space-and-time. We might argue that it is a way of reaching a reality that our cousins, the quadruped mammals, are still in touch with. They have no need of prayer. They do not need – from time to time – to rid themselves of the restlessness of a gigantic neocortex.

The Praying Midwife

The link between praying and giving birth is also implied by the qualities often required to be a traditional midwife in non-industrialised societies. In the 1980s Jacqueline Vincent Priya – originally a market researcher – went to live in Malaysia where she visited a great number of traditional midwives with her baby daughter, who was still breastfeeding. Later she travelled on to Thailand, visiting the Lahu, Akka and the Karen, and in Indonesia went among the Bataks, the Minangkabau and the Toraja. From her enquiries, it seems clear that in order to be a traditional midwife in such societies, a woman needs to have given birth easily herself, and also to pray easily.[1]

Nami, a midwife from the Lahu tribe in northern Thailand, explained with great simplicity how she had become a midwife.

> I gave birth to my children on my own and ... I don't know ... people used to say that as I'd given birth on my own I'd be able to help others. They started coming to me for my help and I suppose I've been doing it for about 20 years now.

This is food for thought for people who go about selecting women who want to enter a modern midwifery school!

Although many midwives visited by Jacqueline Vincent Priya mentioned praying and 'communicating with the spirits' as a way to assist a labouring woman, they were unwilling to disclose details about their prayers. They obviously considered praying an aspect of their private life, as Buleh, a Malaysian midwife claimed: 'I cannot reveal the special prayers that I use as they are confidential between me and the spirit.' Praying and giving birth are again seen as intensely private events which effectively keep the human community at a distance.

These days, there is an urgent need to go back to the roots of midwifery and we should think about the main qualities of the more traditional birth attendants. Typical modern midwives have had a long training and become experts selected according to their highly specialised knowledge, but they have few points in common with midwives who came to the work because other women in the community felt secure with them. Being a mother who has given birth easily seems to be as good a yardstick as any to judge a woman's ability to be a midwife. An ability to change one's level of consciousness at the same time as the labouring woman fits perfectly with our understanding of birth physiology – a midwife who is deep in her own prayer does not disturb the labouring woman to the same degree as someone who behaves like an observer or an expert guide. These traditional qualities are not incompatible with the acquisition of the sort of basic knowledge we deem necessary for midwives in our society at the moment.

Similar Obstacles

The main obstacles to understanding the physiology of genuine spontaneous prayer are the same as the obstacles that stand in the way of our understanding birth physiology. Both events tend to be regulated by human communities. Around childbirth, the community usually interferes by denying the mother's need of privacy, by imposing its own rituals and by handing down its particular beliefs. As for prayer, it is more or less regulated by all religions, especially the four prophetic religions. For example, male Jews must recite the Schema twice a day, while the Islamic Salat is performed five times a day, the supplicant turning towards Mecca in a strictly specified posture. Although the religions of non-literate people also channel the human need to pray, certain forms of spontaneous prayer have been found, for example, among the Negritos of the Philippines and the Alacaluf of Tierra del Fuego.[2]

Thus, we can only extrapolate and try to imagine what was originally a pure, genuine, spontaneous instinctive way of praying. In spite of similar difficulties in the realms of child-birth, perhaps it is easier at the end of the twentieth century to have a clear vision of what is universal in the birth process. Some women can reach such an instinctive state when they are giving birth that, whatever their original cultural milieu, the similarities in their behaviour are much more striking than the differences. We can learn from particular cases, such as a young single mother giving birth unobserved in her own bathroom. We are so ignorant of birth physiology and the physiology of praying that we should not scorn any new approach, and one new avenue we might explore is the connections between apparently unrelated aspects of our lives.

Just as birth physiology can be better understood when studied in relation to other episodes of our sexual life, it is also profitable to look at the birth process and the act of prayer as two closely related topics. This approach helps us to realise that the social human being needs to escape from her condition as a 'person' now and then. The word 'person' indicates the image of ourselves we present to the community, and comes from the Latin 'persona' which is the mask used by someone playing a part as an actor.

A human being cannot be a 'person' all the time. It would be exhausting. In some circumstances it might be health threaten-ing. There are times when we need to lose contact with the community, to be ourselves, to have privacy and to feel humble; in other words we need to reduce the degree of neocortical control which is usually exercised in our everyday lives. The need for prayer is at its height in early adulthood at a time when the neocortex is fully developed. Praying is the way back towards our mammalian roots. At least in the figurative sense, it implies bending forward. The original reason for praying may have been to occasionally remove the mask we usually present to the world.

Likewise, giving birth is typically a situation in which a woman has an absolute need to drop her mask, to stop being a 'person'. In privacy and with humility, the labouring woman accepts her mammalian condition. She needs to bend forward ...

Summary

The connection between giving birth and praying is suggested by the image of a labouring woman 'going to another planet', on her hands and knees. Praying and giving birth are presented as intensely private events which effectively keep the human community at a distance.

References

1 Priya, Jacqueline Vincent *Birth without doctors*. Earthscan, London, 1991.
2 'Forms of prayer in the religions of the world.' In *Encyclopaedia Britannica* 15th edn, Chicago, 1994: 783.

16   The Scientification of Forgiveness

The capacity to forgive may be presented as a facet of the capacity to love. Forgiveness has been held as an important virtue by most societies throughout history and around the world. This facet of the capacity to love is of paramount importance at a time when Humanity must invent new strategies for survival. The necessary dialogue between Humanity and Mother Earth remains impossible as long as old conflicts between ethnic groups and nations are not overcome. Developing the capacity to forgive is the prerequisite to entering a new phase in the history of our species.

A New Phenomenon

The scientific study of forgiveness developed during the very last years of the twentieth century. There was a landmark in October 1997. At that time the John Templeton Foundation invited more than forty scholars to participate in a conference in Holland, Michigan, in order to initiate forgiveness research and to establish a grant programme.[1]

This landmark was made possible thanks to preliminary steps in 1992. Two teams then independently placed at the disposal of researchers psychometric instruments for measuring forgiveness. The Enright Forgiveness Inventory (EFI) is a 60-item scale. It has a scoring range of 60–360, with higher scores indicating greater forgiveness. The tests developed by Mauger are unique in that they attempt to measure forgiveness as a trait rather than as a response to an isolated interpersonal offence. They have a special interest in the framework of our study of the scientification of love because they distinguish the capacity to forgive others and the capacity to forgive oneself: the 'FOO scale' measures 'forgiveness of others' while the 'FOS scale' measures 'forgiveness of self'.[2] These measures are included as subscales of a larger personality inventory, the 'Behavioral Assessment System' (BAS). Until now researchers have mostly used the Enright inventory.

The published studies of the capacity to forgive can be classified into three groups according to their objectives. Some tried to test the efficacy of a therapeutic intervention. Others studied forgiveness as a psychotherapeutic goal. Others examined the relation of forgiveness to other personality traits such as anxiety, depression, religiosity and social desirability.

Each group can be illustrated by an example of published study.

Examples

A study by Coyle and Enright belongs to the first group. The objective was to test the efficacy of a therapy within a sample of men who identified themselves as being hurt by their female partner's decision to have an abortion.[3] The average time span between the abortion and study participation was six years. One group was randomly assigned to participate immediately in a personalised specific psychotherapy that included a series of twelve 90-minute sessions. The other group was on a waiting list for twelve weeks. Before and after the therapy, the participants completed a series of tests, including the Enright Forgiveness Inventory; the other tests consisted of the state anger scale, the state anxiety scale, a perinatal grief scale and a self-forgiveness scale. According to this study an intervention designed to promote forgiveness has therapeutic benefits in excess of what could be expected through the passage of time and repeated testing alone.

A study by Hebl and Enright belongs to the second group. Women participating in this study were over 65 (mean age 74½).[4] They had reported a specific, painful forgiveness issue and were not currently grieving over a major loss. Some of them were randomly assigned to group therapies focusing on the concept of forgiveness. Others participated in free discussions on non-specific subjects. In both cases the sessions were an hour long and repeated over the course of eight weeks. Before and after the series, all participants completed tests measuring anxiety, depression and self-esteem. At the end of the series they were tested with a simplified 30-item version of the Enright Forgiveness Inventory. They also completed a 16-item test called the 'willingness-to-forgive scale'. Both the experimental and the control groups appear to have been therapeutic for participants. However, the experimental group appears to have met its goal of increasing forgiveness in its participants. Forgiveness in turn was associated with greater mental health within the entire sample.

A study by Subkoviak and colleagues belongs to the third group. The objective was to study the relation of forgiveness to anxiety, depression, religiosity and social desirability.[5] Half the sample consisted of 394 college students (204 females and 190 males. Their mean age was 22. The other half consisted of their same-gender parents (mean age 50). Participants were asked to recall the most recent experience of being hurt deeply and unfairly by someone. They then completed the Enright Forgiveness Inventory. They also completed other tests assessing their anxiety, their sociability and their religiosity. Forgiveness was associated with lower anxiety scores, a relationship that was especially strong for students experiencing deep hurt. No significant correlations with depression were found. The student group appeared to find forgiveness more difficult than the parent group. Although there was no relationship between forgiveness and the seven-item religiosity measure, persons who were affiliated with a religion showed slightly higher levels of forgiveness than those who were not affiliated.

The Future: How the Capacity to Pardon Develops

It is noticeable that the capacity to forgive is the only facet of the capacity to love that researchers have tried to measure. It is also noticeable that until now researchers have not raised the fundamental question: 'How does the capacity to pardon develop?' The Primal Health Research perspective offers new avenues for research. It should be possible today to explore the capacity to love in relation to what the birth was like, to what happened to the mother when she was pregnant, to the mode of infant feeding, etc. Both Primal Health Research and the 'Scientification of Love' are at an early phase of development.

Summary

The capacity to forgive – a facet of the capacity to love – has recently been studied with scientific methods.

References

1 Worthington, E. ed. *Dimensions of forgiveness.* Templeton Foundation Press 1998.
2 Mauger, P.A., Perry, J.E., Freeman, T., et al. 'The measurement of forgiveness: preliminary research.' *J. of Psychology and Christianity* 1992; 11: 170–80.
3 Coyle, C.T. and Enright, R.D. 'Forgiveness intervention with post-abortion men.' *J. of Consulting and Clinical Psychology* 1997; 65: 1042–5.
4 Hebl, J.H. and Enright, R.D. 'Forgiveness as a psychotherapeutic goal with elderly females.' *Psychotherapy* 1993; 30: 658–67.
5 Subkoviak, M.J., Enright, R.D., Wu, C., et al. 'Measuring interpersonal forgiveness in late adolescence and middle adulthood.' *J. of Adolescence* 1995; 18: 641–55.

17 Releasing the Brakes with Water

In our view of sexuality as a whole we emphasised that sexual intercourse, childbirth and lactation can be inhibited by the part of the brain which is highly developed among humans – the neocortex. These neocortical brakes are activated particularly in any situation in which high levels of adrenaline are released. This would be the case in any potentially dangerous situation. It is empirical knowledge that, in a variety of circumstances, the presence of water in the environment tends to 'release the brakes'.

Learning from Women

My own interest in the powerful influence of water on human beings developed at a time when I was exploring how the environment might influence the physiology of birth. It was apparent that many labouring women are attracted to water, wanting to have a shower or a bath. One day I went to a shop in the high street of our town and I bought an inflatable blue children's paddling pool. This was the beginning of the history of hospital birthing pools.[1] As soon as the pool was installed I was faced with the most intriguing aspects of the human fascination with water. I could tell countless stories about labouring women whose attraction to water was so irresistible that they frustrated the best-laid plans of the hospital staff. As soon as the tap was turned on, some of them could not wait to get into the pool and stepped in while there was no more than an inch of water in the bottom. The first lesson we learnt was that while the labouring woman is anticipating getting into the pool – hearing the noise of running water and seeing the blue water in a room that was painted blue with dolphins on the walls – it was as if a brake was already being released.

Beyond Daily Practice

Some time afterwards I began to realise how universal that tremendous attraction to water is during labour. In tropical countries, in places where quiet water was available, women often gave birth close to a river, or a lake or the sea. The aborigines of the west coast of Australia used to walk in shallow water before giving birth on the beach. It is probable that women relaxed and even gave birth in warm calm water in places as far apart as what is today called Columbia and Panama, some of the Polynesian islands, or some of the southern Japanese islands. It is also probable that in countries with non-tropical climates, the attraction to water in labour may have been stifled simply because hot and cold water from the tap was not available. However, this attraction could express itself in other subtle ways. At the beginning of this century, when most babies were born at home, the father used to spend hours boiling water. This ritual could be seen as an unconscious attempt to include water in the process of birth.

The similarities between the mysterious influence of water on the birth process and the erotic power of water are striking.[2] It would take volumes to make an in-depth study about the way in which the erotic power of water has been an inspiration to poets, painters, film makers, novelists, advertising agents or restaurant owners, for example. And where do a young couple dream of going when they plan their honeymoon?

A watery environment also seems to beneficially affect the 'milk ejection reflex'. Certain breastfeeding advisers know how to take advantage of the sound of water. It can help women who have to express their milk with a breast pump if they do it in the shower. What is more, the 'oceanic' feeling of mystical emotions is more likely to manifest itself on a beach, or by a river, or a lake.

Interpreting the Power of Water

It is easy to convince anyone of the mysterious effect of water on our human neocortical brakes. The real questions are: is this effect an aspect of our mammalian condition, or is our powerful relationship with water a specifically human trait? After all, all mammals, including the primates, spend their foetal life in water; yet there are some compelling reasons to claim that humans beings should be studied in depth from that point of view.

Today there is a tendency to consider *Homo* as a primate who adapted to living on the coast during certain phases of the evolutionary process. Any study of human nature should start from one fundamental and inescapable question: what sort of environment was *Homo* originally adapted to?

In the case of other species of mammals in general – and primates in particular – it is easy to answer such a question. It is clear, for example, that the common chimpanzees were originally adapted to the African tropical forest and spent much of their time in the trees, while baboons adapted to the drier areas of Arabia and Africa and lived mainly on the ground. As for *Homo*, scientists can only offer hypotheses and theories.

In the current scientific context, it is well accepted that *Homo* separated from the other chimpanzees about six million years ago. Until recently, the favourite scenario was that our ancestors abandoned life in the trees to live on the open plain. According to the 'Savannah' theory this change of habitat is the crucial factor that precipitated the emergence of *Homo*. Yet today there are many serious reasons to dismiss the 'Savannah' theory – principally because the presumed period for the emergence of savannah conditions in Africa has been reassessed by new dating of the explosion of different species of hoof-footed mammals, pollen analysis and closer examination of fossils of small mammals found in association with fossils of hominids.[3] It appears that the emergence of the savannah occurred after the origin of the human family. Furthermore, we must bear in mind that the bones of our ancestor, the famous Lucy (*Australopithecus Afarensis*) were found eroding from the sand, lying among turtle and crocodile eggs and crab claws. And the bones of an older *Australopithecus*, found near Lake Rudolph in Kenya in 1995 were surrounded by many fossil vertebrates including fish and aquatic reptiles.[4]

We must also keep in mind that even though the human family emerged several million years ago, *Homo sapiens* – the modern human being – is a young species. It is worth noticing that the oldest known footprints of a modern human being – dating back 117,000 years ago – have been found on the shore of a South African lagoon.

At the very time of the collapse of the 'Savannah' theory, an alternative hypothesis – often called the Aquatic Ape theory – is gradually gaining ground and filling the gaps. Quite independently, Max Westenhofer in Berlin (as early as 1942)[5] and Alister Hardy in Oxford in 1960[6] underlined that several of the differences between *Homo* and the other apes suggest an adaptation to a semi-aquatic environment. Since these pioneering works, the Aquatic Ape theory has developed and has been constantly updated thanks to the enthusiastic, creative and persevering work of Elaine Morgan.[7, 8, 9]

Although, from a genetic perspective, we are a sort of chimpanzee (sharing 98.5 per cent of our genes), dozens of features make us different from our close relatives. All these features are compatible with an adaptation to the coast.

Bipedalism – standing, walking and running upright – has been at the root of the theory from the beginning. Both Westenhofer and Hardy suggested that bipedalism was first adopted under duress, by ancestors of the human family confronted by the necessity of wading through water. It is well known that human babies can walk in shallow water before being able to walk on dry land. It is also noticeable that the only primate in the wild who regularly walks on two feet is the proboscis monkey of Borneo – a primate that is frequently constrained to walk in shallow water. One possible scenario among others is that some of our ancestors were isolated on an island when a part of East Africa was covered by the sea.

When ancestors of the human family established bipedalism as their usual mode of locomotion, favourable conditions were met for a dramatic development of the brain. An upright posture is easily compatible with an increased head weight (we can only carry heavy weights on our heads when we are upright). Also, the coastal food chain is the best possible environment in which to find unlimited quantities of all the nutrients that are essential for brain development. Among these nutrients are the long chain omega-3 fatty acids that are abundant and preformed in seafood.[10] As soon as they had access to the coastal food chain our ancestors had an ideal balance of nutrients from the land and from the sea at their disposal, and so could develop their full potential.[11, 12]

In the 1990s a further factor has added its weight to the list of scientific data supporting the Aquatic Ape theory, which is our better knowledge of the specific nutritional needs of the developing brain. Until now it was impossible to explain why the human brain is four times bigger than the brain of other chimpanzees and the fact that, in terms of the proportion of grey matter to the total brain mass, there is no difference between *Homo* and unrelated mammals such as dolphins. One of the most mysterious aspects of human nature for modern biologists is that we have to feed an enormous brain yet our body is not very efficient at making one of the molecules ('DHA') which is essential to meet the needs of the nervous system.

Nakedness has been identified as one of the most specifically human traits since the biblical book of Genesis. It was being discussed as a scientific mystery at the time of Darwin, who rejected the notion that it was our best protection against the many skin parasites found in tropical regions, arguing that, if it was the case, other animals living in the tropics would have rid themselves of their hairy coats to cope with the same problem. In fact, any attempt to interpret human nakedness should start with a reminder of the main function of fur, which is to protect from variations in temperature by maintaining a layer of air around the body. In water there is no need for fur. The absence of hair is a characteristic of most sea-mammals. The only ones that keep their fur are those that can get out of the water and stay on land in a cold climate, such a seals, otters and beavers. Our subcutaneous layer of fat is as mysterious as our naked-ness. It is not a feature we share with other apes although it is a point we have in common with many mammals adapted to the sea. In addition, we sweat in order to control our body temperature, and of all mammals we have the highest sweat production. Sweating has long been considered an enigma, or a mistake of nature as it depletes the body of large amounts of water and salt. This makes no sense at all to those thinkers who see humans, first and foremost, as primates who keep the characteristics of a foetus or a baby until adulthood. (In fact the human baby does not control its temperature by sweating for the first few weeks after birth.) New interpretations of this sweating mechanism become possible when we consider human beings as primates who have adapted to environments where water and salt are freely available. In fact, fur seals are the only other mammals who sweat when they are overheated on land (they sweat on their naked hind flippers). Therefore sweating is yet another human trait that is compatible with adaptation to the coast.

We might focus on many other intriguing human traits such as the triangle of skin we have between our thumbs and forefingers (similar to the webbing on a duck's feet), the fact that our big toes are jointed to the others, the anatomy of our respiratory tract, or the number of blood cells per cubic millimetre. All these features suggest that we are adapted to a semi-aquatic environment.

Another feature peculiar to humans is the expression of emotion with tears. This is not incompatible with an adaptation to the sea, since marine iguanas, turtles, marine crocodiles, sea snakes, seals and sea otters weep salt tears, while land mammals have no tears or any sort of nasal salt gland. The human lachrymal glands might be interpreted as a vestige of an extra mechanism for eliminating salt.

We might also look at one of the main obvious differences when you compare a photo of a man and a photo of a chimpanzee. One has a nose and the other only has two breathing holes. The long nose is a feature we have in common with the proboscis monkey who is a swimmer adapted to the coast.

Another intriguing phenomenon needs interpretation and is also supportive of this new vision of *Homo sapiens*. Consider the fact that the two wonder drugs of the last half of this century are fish oils and aspirin. It has been claimed that these can remedy an astonishing variety of conditions, and in particular, specifically human diseases. Fish oil capsules have been found to reduce the risk or the effects of coronary heart disease, hyper-cholesterolemia, hypertension, psoriasis and other skin diseases, migraines, painful menstruation, different forms of rheumatism, dyslexia, attention deficit disorder, poor adaptation to darkness, allergic diseases, ulcerative colitis, Crohn's disease, pre-eclampsia, foetal growth retardation and even some cancers. As for aspirin, it is undoubtedly the most commonly used medicinal agent in the world, and, like fish oils, can modify the metabolism of an important family of cell regulators called prostaglandins. It is as if a very large number of humans are finding they need the same sort of correction to their metabolism of prostaglandins. Theoretically, from a biochemical point of view, people who have easy access to the sea-food chain would have no need of such correction. Perhaps these modern panaceas offer us a new perspective from which to explore human nature.

This new vision of *Homo sapiens* as an ape adapted to life on the coast represents such a radical change in the current understanding of human nature that it will take a long time to digest it. It signifies another vital aspect of the scientific revolution going on today. It is developing at the same time as the scientification of love. It helps us to understand why human beings feel more secure in a watery environment and enables us to interpret the magic power of water on human beings.

Summary

There are similarities between the erotic power of water, the mysterious power of water on the birth process and the way in which an aquatic environment can be used to facilitate lactation. Water, as a symbol, helps humans to feel secure in a great variety of circumstances. What is the root cause of these cross-cultural effects?

References

1   Odent, M. 'Birth under water.' *Lancet* 1983: 1476–7.
2   Odent, M. *Water and sexuality.* Arkana (Penguin), London, 1990.
3   Leakey, R. and Lewin, R. *Origins reconsidered.* Little, Brown, Boston, 1992.

4 Leakey, M.G. et al. 'New four million year old hominid species.' *Nature* 1995; 376: 565–71.

5 Westenhofer, M. *Der Eigenweg des menschen.* Mannstaede and Co., Berlin, 1942.

6 Hardy, A. 'Was Man more aquatic in the past?' *New Scientist* 1960; 7: 642–5.

7 Morgan, E. *The descent of woman.* Souvenir Press, London, 1972.

8 Morgan, E. *The aquatic ape.* Souvenir Press, London, 1982.

9 Morgan, E. *The scars of evolution.* Souvenir Press, London, 1990.

10 Crawford, M. and Marsh, D. *The driving force.* Heinemann, London, 1989.

11 Odent, M., McMillan, L. and Kimmel, T. 'Prenatal care and seafish.' *Eur. J. Obstet. Gynecol.* 1996; 68: 49–51.

12 Odent, M. 'The primary human disease: an evolutionary perspective.' *ReVision* 1995; 18, 2: 19–21.

18 Love at a Molecular Level

'We'll gain in knowledge of emotional states when scientists study love at a molecular level.' Twenty years ago I would not have imagined that such an assumption could become scientifically justified.

Today I do not hesitate to claim that 'the Love Hormone induces the release of the Heart Hormone'. If I had written such a thing in the 1980s – in the middle ages of the scientification of love – I would have been certified crazy. It is not so around the year 2000. Now, calling oxytocin the hormone of love is based upon scientific evidence and it has been demonstrated that oxytocin stimulates the release of a chemical messenger called the 'atrial natriuretic peptide' by certain heart cells.[1]

I offer these peremptory facts to convince everyone that we must first change our perspectives by starting all over again to introduce a new mind set and make the most of a new generation of research.

Beyond the Brain

Until recently, the physiological studies of emotional states were exclusively the province of brain researchers. In the 1980s it was fashionable to explore and to map the emotive circuits of the brain and to induce a great variety of emotional responses by stimulating precise zones of the primitive parts of the brain. Due emphasis was placed on the knowledge that the emotional wiring develops early in the evolution of the mammalian brain; it was well accepted that the key to elaborating fruitful theories about the emotions was to make an in-depth study of the brain structures that we share with all mammals (the limbic system). At that time it was as if the scientists interested in emotional states were stuck in the 'limbic system'.

In the 1990s the tendency to only consider the physiology of emotional states in the context of brain physiology has been reinforced by the development of sophisticated techniques of brain imaging. For example, with 'Positron Emission Tomography' (PET) it is possible to identify the brain areas that are working hardest by measuring their fuel intake, whereas 'Functional Magnetic Resonance Imaging' can show up the areas where there is the most oxygen. However, it also came about in the 1990s that the emotional brain circuits were more commonly seen as a part of the complex network that I call the 'primal adaptive system'.

The nature of emotions cannot be understood as long as the focus is only on the brain. We must get rid of our previous simplistic visions of organs associated with functions. Our deep-rooted simplistic visions are understandable: anatomy is an old science and physiology a new one. The time has come for a divorce.

In the past the heart was given one precise function, i.e. it was just a pump. Today we know that specialised heart cells can release 'informational substances'. In the past the gut was an organ where food is digested and where the nutrients are absorbed. Today it may be seen also as a most complex endocrine gland.

In the current scientific context the physiologists who inspire a renewed understanding of emotional states are those who study the interactions between 'informational substances' and their receptors.

Receptors, Informational Substances and Binding Sites

Receptors are molecules of proteins that act at a cellular level. They cluster in the cellular membranes or inside the cells, waiting for the right 'informational substance' to reach them so that they can bind to it. This phenomenon of selective attraction and 'binding' can be seen as love at a molecular level. The appropriate word to refer to these 'informational substances' that bind selectively to their receptors is 'ligand', from Latin *'ligare'*, which means 'to tie up'. To understand the nature and the role of these ligands it is necessary, once more, to turn everything upside down, including the vocabulary. Even terms such as 'hormones', 'endocrine system' or 'immune system' are confusing. In 1986 I already felt the need for a simple appropriate term to avoid the use of awkward phrases such as the 'psychoneuroimmunoendocrinological system'. I suggested the term 'primal adaptive system'. The term 'primal' (first in time and first in importance) stresses that this network reaches a high degree of maturity as early as during the 'primal period', that is from conception until the first birthday.[2] Hundreds of ligands have already been identified. From a chemical point of view they can be classified in two groups. Some of them are steroids, which means that the parent molecule is cholesterol. This group includes the corticosteroids, such as cortisol, re-leased by the adrenal gland, and also sex hormones such as testosterone, oestrogens and progesterone. The steroids act on receptors located in the nucleus of the cells. All of them are hormones according to the old classification. Other ligands are peptides, made from the association of amino acids. They act on the receptors located on the surface of the cells. Some of them are very small molecules, made of one or a small number of amino acids. This is the case of the ligands which carry information between nerve cells. Acetylcholine or dopamine are examples. They are usually classified at 'neurotransmitters'. Other peptides are more complex and associate a greater number of amino acids. For example oxytocin and vasopressin associate nine amino acids. These more complex peptides are usually classified as hormones.

The Faithfulness of Ligands

Today hundreds of research teams are in the process of studying the attraction between all these informational sub-stances and their specific receptors and of tracing the 'binding sites'. A brilliant overview of this promising generation of research has already been offered by Candace Pert,[3] the neuroscientist who discovered in 1973 the existence of opiate receptors in the brain, and opened the way to the discovery of the so-called 'endorphins'. Let us emphasise that our analogy is reinforced by one of the main characteristics of the ligands: they are faithful; they talk to their own receptors only.

It would be irrelevant, in our simplified introduction to the scientification of love, to mention details which are only understandable by a small circle of experts. Such experts in this fast-moving field are highly specialised. However, a short review of their relevant research projects informs the scientification of love.

The Case of Oxytocin

If we consider, for example, the case of oxytocin receptors, we realise that a great diversity of research teams are at work. Some study the oxytocin receptors in the uterine muscle. The practical implications of such studies are obvious. It is generally believed that an increased sensitivity to oxytocin is fundamental for initiation of labour at term. This increased sensitivity seems to be regulated by an increase in oxytocin binding sites. A Swedish team obtained a tiny piece of uterine muscle from 50 women undergoing caesarean section for a great diversity of reasons.[4] Some of them were not in labour, others were in the active phase of spontaneous labour, others had a 'failure to progress', others could give birth with a drip of oxytocin, others could not give birth even with a drip of oxytocin. The first conclusion was that the number of binding sites was smaller among those women who were not in labour. The second conclusion was that women who had a caesarean section because of 'failure to progress' or because they had an 'oxytocin resistant labour' also had a smaller number of oxytocin receptors.

Such results inspire questions and speculations. One can wonder why women are not equal in developing oxytocin receptors during labour. One can speculate that previous opportunities to release high levels of oxytocin facilitates the development of a greater number of receptors during labour. From that point of view, it would be useful to compare women who give birth to a first baby and women who have previously given birth and breastfed a child. One can even speculate that self-exploration, flirting and sexual intercourse are ways to prepare the uterine muscle.

Other research teams trace the oxytocin receptors involved in the release of prostaglandins during labour. Their fields of research are the mucous membrane of the uterus (the 'endometrium'), the placenta[5] and the amnion,[6] that is to say the innermost membrane enclosing the foetus.

Others study the breast receptors. Since oxytocin is necessary for the 'milk ejection reflex' it is not surprising to find a high density of receptors in the breast.

There are also neuroscientists who have a special interest in the oxytocin receptors in different brain areas. Oxytocin receptors in the brain resemble those described in uterus and breast. They have been identified in several regions of the primitive brain. Among rats there is an increased number of oxytocin receptors during birth in a particular brain zone usually called BNST ('bed nucleus of the stria terminalis').[7] Because the experimental destruction of this zone inhibits maternal behaviour without disturbing the birth, it appears that the oxytocin receptors of that zone play an important role in maternal behaviour. The studies of love at a molecular level confirm that oxytocin is a major love hormone.

At the end of this quick and superficial review of a promising generation of research, the point is to realise that *avant-garde* physiological studies of emotional states – including emotions associated with all our infinite variety of feelings of love – must look beyond the brain. Today physiologists offer us new ways to interpret the intriguing cross-cultural double meaning of the word 'heart'. They also help us to understand why we have 'gut feelings'.

Summary

Specialised experts in one of the fast-moving fields of molecular biology study how receptors attract the right informational substances to the right 'binding sites'. Today emotional states – when studied by physiologists – are not exclusively the province of brain researchers. Our view of the functions of such organs as the heart or the gut is dramatically enlarged.

References

1 Gutkowska, J., Antunes-Rodrigues, J. and McCann, S.M. 'Atrial natriuretic peptide in brain and pituitary gland.' *Physiological Review* 1997; 77; 2: 465–515.
2 Odent, M. *Primal health*. Century Hutchinson, London, 1986.
3 Pert, C. *Molecules of emotion*. Scribner, London, 1997.
4 Rezapour, M., Bäckström, T. and Ulmstem, V. 'Myometrial steroid concentration and oxytocin receptor density in parturient women at term.' *Steroids* 1996; 61: 338–44.
5 Fuchs, A.R., Hussein, P. and Fuchs, F. 'Oxytocin and the initiation of human parturition. Stimulation of prostaglandin production in human decidua by oxytocin.' *Am. J. Obstet. Gynecol.* 1981; 141: 694–7.
6 Solof, M. and Hinko, A. 'Oxytocin receptor and prostaglandin release in rabbit amnion.' In North, W.G. and Moses, A.M. eds *The Neurohypophysis. Annals of the New York Academy of Sciences.* 1993; 689: 207–18.
7 Insel, T.R. and Shapiro, L.E. 'Oxytocin receptors and maternal behavior.' In Pedersen, C.A. et al. eds *Oxytocin in maternal, sexual and social behaviors. Annals of the New York Academy of Sciences.* 1992; 652: 122–41.

'Babyist' Interlude 1:
The Twenty-Second Century from
the Baby's Perspective

The most important lesson to be learnt from the scientification of love is that we cannot prepare for the future without embracing the meaning and the relevance of the baby's perspective on life. Up till now our societies have been 'adultist' – only the adult view of the world has been taken seriously. In order to educate ourselves for such a radical change I suggest that we open an imaginary history textbook written from the baby's point of view. Topics which we now ignore or overlook because we regard them as unimportant, inconsequential or taboo will be seen as serious and crucial issues.

A Futuristic History Textbook

It would take volumes to speculate about such issues as the phenomenon of wet nurses, for example. A 2,000-year chunk of humankind's history will be seen as a time when a great number of babies, born to wealthy families, had two mothers during their 'primal period' – one mother during the intrauterine phase, and another during the extrauterine phase. Moreover, the second mother was a kind of mercenary, earning her living by producing milk and (optionally) giving love.

As a baby might see it, a turning point in the history of humankind occurred in the millennium preceding the birth of Jesus, with the advent of modern family structures. What was to lead later on to the nuclear family was originally a Greek-Roman-Middle Eastern phenomenon. As soon as life-long strict monogamy was introduced as the only morally acceptable marital arrangement, the tendency was to reduce the duration of breastfeeding and to find substitutes for the mother's milk in the form of nursing slaves, wet nurses, animal milk and finally condensed or powdered milk and a variety of 'formulas'. High-class women in Greek society were afraid of neglecting their 'duties' and their babies were fed by slaves called *'titthai'*. Tacitus, who was a contemporary of Jesus, contrasted the moral laxity of the Romans with the simple virtues of German tribes. In his writings he criticised the reluctance of Roman mothers to nurse their babies while German mothers were breastfeeding for periods of several years.[1]

If we focus on the history of the Hebrews we might conclude that radical changes took place over a period of four centuries between the reign of King Solomon and the destruction of Jerusalem by the Babylonians. It is significant that, as early as the sixth century BC, when Jeremiah called for moral reform in his 'Lamentations', the issue of infant feeding was already expressed in quasi-modern terms: 'Even the jackals draw out the breast, they give suck to their young. The daughter of my people is becoming cruel...'[2] Among Jews of that time, it would have been clear that 'even the jackals' meant 'even the most aggressive, carnivorous animals you can imagine'.

We are constantly and subtly reminded that infant feeding and genital sexuality are closely related topics. The Koran gives a good example. It specifies that the breastfeeding period is two years,[3] ... but weaning can be allowed earlier if the father and mother mutually consent to curtailing this term. It is worth emphasising that, in the framework of our main monotheistic religions, the Koran is the only collection of writings which attaches importance to the duration of breastfeeding – and the Koran does not consider strict monogamy to be the only morally acceptable marital arrangement. However, the Koran condemns intercourse during pregnancy and whilst breastfeeding as morally unacceptable, and this would have influenced behaviour in a society where it was quite acceptable for a man to have more than one wife.

From old texts about wet nurses, and particularly in a detailed 'Memoires' from Florence in the fourteenth century, it seems that the time for weaning was discussed mostly between the father of the baby and the husband of the wet nurse, in much the same way that they would have discussed the financial arrangements between them.[4] It is as if wealthy men had the power to convert maternal love into sexual love for their own benefit.

When an exclusively adult point of view is put aside, the history of a country like Iceland grows more significant. Iceland is probably the place where the tendency to reduce the duration of breastfeeding and introduce substitutes for human milk had become most extreme. In fact, by the end of the nineteenth century, Icelandic babies had not been breastfed at all for about two centuries[5] and this had been possible thanks to the use of a variety of breastmilk substitutes including chewed fish – a dietary item which helped to introduce fatty acids that are essential for brain development. At that time many Icelandic women had more than a dozen children. According to Bishop Oddur Einarsson, many women were giving birth to 20 or 30 children at the end of the sixteenth century. Until the late nineteenth century the death rate of infants was 300–400 per 1,000; Iceland is probably the only country in the world which could maintain its population over a period of several centuries without babies being given any human milk at all. This process of survival of the fittest has been so harsh and pitiless than now the Icelandics are among the healthiest people on the planet.

Biographical literature, which is currently seen as the most popular depiction of history, could be dramatically influenced by new perspectives. Biographies line the shelves of bookshops. Glance through some at random and you will find that most biographers demonstrate a surprising lack of interest and curiosity about their subject's 'primal period'. One of the first examples of a modern biography – 'Life of Jesus' by Ernest Renan published in 1863[6] – was an historical study of Jesus which mentions the probable year of his birth (the year 750 in Rome) and probable place of birth (Nazareth), before launching into details of a 'life' which starts with childhood and education in a certain socio-cultural environment. This is typical of modern work by biographers who rarely think of researching the circumstances of conception, what happened to the mother while she was pregnant, details of the birth itself, or early infancy. Of course there are anecdotal exceptions – Napoleon was 'born in his caul' while the church bells were ringing!

A Futuristic Encyclopaedia

Nowadays well-known encyclopaedias have entries like 'lullaby' which are more often than not ignored. In a futuristic encyclopaedia 'lullaby' might cover pages, with numerous subheadings. The topic will become so vast that the editor will need the cooperation of a multi-disciplinary team – experts in human development will evaluate the role of sensory stimulation associated with lullabies; experts in brain asymmetry will explain why most mothers cradle their baby on the left hand side when singing lullabies; physiologists will explore the transition from a waking state to a sleeping state; anthropologists will detect common factors and differences between cultures; musicologists will study the relationship between lullabies and other sorts of song and music; linguists will report on the results of their research into the role of lullabies in the transmission of language, etc.

Others will interpret the gradual disappearance of lullabies. Some years ago I went to Kabylie in the Berber part of Algeria in order to participate in a documentary film about birth traditions and babies. While an 80-year-old woman was able to sing traditional local lullabies, her granddaughters, young mothers in their twenties, were busy making pancakes. They still knew how to make the traditional pancakes but were unable to sing lullabies.

In the same way, let's imagine what the entry 'taste' might be like in the encyclopaedia of the future. There might be long paragraphs about the development of the sense of taste among breastfed babies. The taste of human milk is never the same. It is not the same in the first days after birth and then later on. Foremilk does not taste the same as hindmilk. Morning milk differs from evening milk. These differences come about as a result of what the mother has been eating. On the other hand, formula milk remains exactly the same from the first drop to the last, whatever the time of day. Of course, the sense of taste starts to develop long before birth because the taste of the amniotic fluid which the baby swallows in the womb also reflects the diet of the mother. People who will become familiar with this sort of futuristic encyclopaedia will easily realise how cultural particularities have developed, and why they have tended to fade out at the dawn of the twenty-first century.

Looking Back to our Time

In future, people looking back at this time as we approach the millennium will regard it as one of the great turning points of history from the babies' perspective. This same perspective allows us to look at the current rapid evolution of family structures in an unbiased way. Strict monogamy is still seen as the only acceptable form of marriage by most people in authority, but a new perspective helps us to look more objectively at family structures that are becoming commonplace. 'One-parent' families and 'serial monogamy' (when one person cohabits with a spouse during a certain phase of his or her life, and then with another during another phase) are typical examples. In a study of marital arrangements from the babies' point of view, such new concepts will transcend the traditional restrictive opposition between polygamy and monogamy.

This objective new view may lead to unpopular and slightly scandalous conclusions. That is why this chapter is an interlude which should not be presented too abruptly to anyone who grew up in an 'adultist' society.

References

1 Tacitus. *De origine et situ Germanorum*. AD 98.
2 Lamentations 4: 3–4.
3 Koran, Surat II (Bagara), Verse 233.
4 Klapiszh-Zuber, C. *Genitori naturali e genitori di latte nella Firenze del Quattrocento*. Quadermi storici, Firenze, 1980: 543–63.
5 Hastrup, Kirsten 'A question of reason: breastfeeding patterns in 17th- and 18th-century Iceland.' In Maher, Vanessa ed. *The anthropology of breastfeeding*. Berg, Oxford, 1992: 91–108.
6 Renan, Ernest *Vie de Jesus*, 13ème édition. Le Seuil, Paris, 1992.

'Babyist' Interlude 2:
Don't Bite your Mum!

Twelve recommendations for being breastfed successfully (with the permission of 'Babies Anonymous'):

1   Choose your country of birth carefully. If you are born in Denmark, for example, you are twice as likely to be breastfed successfully than if you are born in France.

2   Choose your grandmother carefully. You are more likely to be breastfed contentedly if your maternal grandmother breastfed her children, particularly your mother.

3   Choose your mother carefully. You are more likely to be breastfed easily if your mum was able, given the opportunity, to give birth without drugs and intervention.

4   Be assertive from the very beginning. Try to find the breast as early as possible after being born, ideally during your first hour outside the womb.

5   Avoid anywhere that has an aggressive smell. Your sense of smell is the best conductor towards the nipple, and one of your first ways of identifying your mum.

6   Spend plenty of time as naked as possible, in close, skin-to-skin contact with your mum.

7   Keep your hands free so that you can touch your mum's body while sucking. There is a hand–mouth connection.

8 Choose the family bed carefully. If the bed is low, you and your mum will feel more secure. Your mum will not be obsessed with the fear that you might fall out. If the bed is wide enough, there might be a little space for another member of the family, such as your dad.

9 Always express your needs clearly. As soon as your mum perceives what they are, she starts to release oxytocin which triggers her 'milk ejection reflex'.

10 When your mum has eaten something you don't like, let her know.

11 Constantly remind your mum about the fast development of your brain. This might influence her diet.

12 Don't bite your mum when your first teeth grow.

Linguistic Note:
About the Suffix '-ation'

Our preliminary definition of the scientification of love was based on the fact that love is becoming a scientific subject. Language experts would probably argue that the suffix '-ation' indicates an action that tends to transform the nature and expression of love.

The conclusions of this book lead us to accept also the definition favoured by the purists.

19 Science–Tradition Convergence

The scientification of love represents the perfect example of the convergence between recent scientific concepts and stories, beliefs, statements and teachings that have been passed down orally from generation to generation since early times.

A Well-Known Example – The Tao of Physics

The interest in the current trend towards science–tradition convergence was originally stimulated by the development of modern physics. Fritjof Capra is a physicist and writer who underlined the similarities between the concepts of modern theoretical physics and eastern traditions.[1] The principles of quantum physics lead us to the conclusion that we cannot 'decompose' the world into what he called 'independently existing elementary units' because the nature of the whole is always different from the mere sum of its parts. Subatomic particles – electrons, protons and neutrons – have no meaning as isolated entities but can be understood only as interconnections. Depending on how we look at them, they sometimes appear to be particles, sometimes waves. This dual nature is also exhibited by light which can take the form of electromagnetic waves or particles. Capra summed it up when he wrote 'in quantum theory we never end up with any "things"; we always deal with interconnections'.[2]

The Buddha also taught that we tend to divide the world as we perceive it into separate objects that we then regard as firm and permanent but which are actually transient and ever changing. All fixed forms such as things, events, people or ideas are nothing more than 'maya' – that is to say, intellectual concepts that have no reality.

Intriguing Similarities

The scientification of love prompts us to reconsider old messages more than any other modern scientific movement. In the current scientific context, we are encouraged to look at old legends about people whose names have been associated with love from a new perspective. The names of Aphrodite, the goddess of love, of Buddha and of Jesus are the first to come to mind.

When re-examining such legends we realise that stories like these are disseminated through a process of natural selection, like all living organisms. When legends are passing on valuable messages about human nature they are evidently more likely to spread and survive over the centuries. Looking back over many old legends, they seem to be a way that human groups have kept old messages alive through time although, in the past, they did not have all the keys to decode them.

One of the main conclusions one can draw from scientific perspectives is that the capacity to love is determined, to a great extent, by early experiences during foetal life and in the period surrounding birth. In light of this important insight, there is a striking similarity between the legends of those people whose names have been associated with love.

The first conspicuous similarity is the way that the circumstances of their conception and how they were born has become an important part of the legend. Biographers of famous people rarely think of researching what happened to their subject's mother when she was pregnant, and they almost never consider the birth itself. Only those people who have realised the relevance of the concept of critical periods in our lives (that has been introduced and discussed within several scientific disciplines in recent years), can easily grasp how obvious the resemblance between the births of Aphrodite, Buddha and Jesus is. These three legendary people were all born outside the human community. This is a highly significant detail when we consider how all known cultures tend to disturb the physiological processes in the period around birth, particularly interfering with the first contact between the mother and baby with a variety of peculiar rituals or beliefs.

The kind of message that is transmitted through a story about a birth in a stable suddenly becomes clear in the age of the scientification of love. Buddha was also born outside the human community in the Lumbini Garden while his mother, Maya, was travelling and had taken a rest among the Ashoka blossoms. In delight she reached her right arm out to pluck a branch and, at that moment, Buddha was born. As for Aphrodite, she was born in the sea, from the foam of the waves.

These sort of concordant messages are not limited to the birth itself, because these three legendary figures were miraculously conceived. Aphrodite was conceived when Cronus severed the testicles of his father Uranus and threw them into the sea. The conception of Buddha was also extraordinary. After twenty years of sterility, Maya had a strange dream in which she saw a white elephant entering into her womb through the right side of her chest, and so she became pregnant. The conception of Jesus was as miraculous as the conception of John the Baptist by Elizabeth the Barren after a visitation by the Angel Gabriel. Evidently these conceptions occurred outside the realm of space and time reality. They occurred whilst the women were in ecstatic states. In the light of modern biological sciences the Holy Spirit might be interpreted as the sense of belonging, being part of the whole, as a state of mind that can be reached when our neocortical computer (and its vision of the universe limited to space and time) is switched off. Being in an orgasmic state is a way to reach a new 'wholy', transcendental dimension.

The circumstances of a conception are an indication of what the emotional state of the mother was like during her pregnancy. In the case of Buddha and Jesus, pregnancy and birth are clearly presented in the legends as a blessing: 'Rejoice, highly favoured one ... blessed are you among women ...' . And when Buddha was born we hear 'Heaven and Earth rejoiced'.

I want to focus on three well-known legends representative of three different cultural backgrounds. Other significant examples might be cited. There are numerous supernatural conceptions in Greek mythology. The mother of Asklepios was miraculously impregnated by the god Apollo. Asklepios (destined to express his compassion by finding remedies for all diseases and become the god of medicine) was born on a mountain and found by a shepherd between a goat and a dog surrounded by a dazzling light.

In a great diversity of cultures, legendary and divine persons were conceived miraculously. As early as the seventeenth century BC, an Egyptian tale engraved on the wall of a temple, tells of the wondrous conception of a Queen. Amon, the Magnificent God, took on the appearance of the King (who was not yet pubescent) and so the heiress of the throne was conceived while the Queen was in an ecstatic state.

They also had such legends in ancient China – Pei Han, a supernatural being, appeared as human and gave a luminous object to the wife of a king – and so a son was conceived.

The Best Book on Birth Physiology

When I refer to the widespread cultural misunderstanding of birth physiology I am often asked for references of reliable articles from journals or textbooks. My answer – usually most unexpected – is to refer people to the only book on the market that can help us to understand the physiological processes in the period around birth. This is a bestseller and was written several millennia ago. On the very first pages there is an intriguing and significant association made. The authors mention the sin of consuming the fruits of the tree of knowledge (that is to say, the sin of knowing too much) and, on the same page, they refer to the fact that human beings are condemned to give birth with difficulty. This link indicates that the development of our intellect is a handicap in certain circumstances in life, particularly when giving birth. I would add that at the end of the same book there is a legend about a man whose mission was to promote love amongst his fellow human beings. His mother found a strategy to cope with a potential handicap and to reduce the activity of her thinking mind when her baby gave the right signal. She gave birth in a stable, among other mammals, separated from the human community. This is one of the best examples we can offer to anyone to illustrate how modern science can help us to unlock old messages.

Projects

A great variety of old messages, such as metaphors and legends may be re-examined and reinterpreted in light of recent scientific advances. Since we are in the Judeo-Christian world, in future I may be tempted to reconsider, in particular, the legend of Jesus. I anticipate difficulties. It is not easy to refer to the life of Jesus and remain outside the fields of religion or history. However, what I am interested in is the wider vision of Jesus as it has been passed down over time, not only by the scriptures and the various churches, but also by painters, poets, musicians and other artists up to the present day rock opera singers.

Summary

Until now, the similarities between the concepts of modern theoretical physics and eastern traditions have been our best representation of the science–tradition convergence. Upon re-examining the legends about people whose names have become associated with love, we discover other fascinating aspects of this convergence. These legendary persons had miraculous conceptions and the way they were born is a significant aspect of their legends. They were all born outside the human community.

As a preliminary exercise I will let my imagination go and offer my own vision of the nativity.

References

1 Capra, F. *The Tao of Physics*. Shambhala, Berkeley, 1975.
2 Capra, F. *The Web of Life*. HarperCollins, London, 1996.

Interlude 3:
Nativity Revisited

Until now the image of the Nativity that has come down to us has usually been restricted to a birth in a stable, in the presence of an ox and a donkey. My vision of the Nativity is inspired by what I have learned from women who have given birth in privacy. It has also been inspired by 'Evangelium Jacobi Minori', the protogospel of James, the brother of Jesus. This gospel was saved from oblivion in the middle of the nineteenth century by the Austrian mystic Jacob Lorber, who wrote *Die Jugend Jesu* (The childhood of Jesus).[1]

According to these texts Mary had complete privacy when giving birth because Joseph had left her to find a midwife. When he returned with a midwife, Jesus had already been born. It was only when a dazzling light had faded that the midwife realised she was facing an incredible scene: Jesus had already found his mother's breast! Then the midwife said: 'Who has ever seen a hardly born baby taking his mother's breast? This is an obvious sign that when he becomes a man, this child will judge the world according to Love and not according to the Law!'

On the day when Jesus was ready to enter the world, Mary was sent a message – a non-verbal message of humility. She found herself in a stable, among other mammals. Without words, her companions helped her to understand that on that day, she had to accept her mammalian condition. She had to cope with her human handicap and disregard the effervescence of her intellect. She had to release the same hormones as other parturient mammals, through the same gland, i.e. the primitive part of the brain that we all have in common.

The environment was ideally adapted to the circumstances. Mary felt secure and, because of this, her level of adrenaline was as low as possible. Labour could establish itself in the best possible conditions. Having perceived the message of humility and accepted her mammalian conditions, Mary found herself on all fours. In a posture like this, and in the darkness of the night, she could easily cut herself off from the everyday world.

Soon after his birth, the newborn Jesus was in the arms of an ecstatic mother, as instinctive as a non-human mammal can be. He was welcomed in an unviolated sacred atmosphere and was able, easily and gradually, to eliminate the high level of stress hormones he had produced while being born. Mary's body was warm. The stable, too, was warm, thanks to the presence of the other mammals. Instinctively Mary covered her baby with a piece of cloth she had on hand. She was fascinated by the baby's eyes and nothing could distract her from prolonged eye-to-eye contact with Jesus. Gazing at each other like this would have been instrumental in inducing another rush of oxytocin, so that her uterus contracted again and returned a small amount of enriched blood from the placenta along the umbilical cord to the baby; and soon after, the placenta was delivered.

Mother and baby could feel quite secure. Mary, guided by her mammalian brain, stayed on her knees for a short while after the birth. After the placenta was delivered she lay down on her side with the baby close to her heart. Suddenly Jesus began to turn his head from one side to the other, opening his mouth into a round O. Guided by his sense of smell, he came closer and closer to the nipple while Mary, who was still in a very special hormonal balance and still behaving very instinctively, knew how to hold the baby and made the right sort of movements to help her baby find the breast.

This is how Mary and Jesus transgressed the rules that had been established by the human community. Jesus, as a peaceful rebel who defied convention, was initiated by his mother. Jesus spent a long time sucking vigorously. With the support of Mary he was able to emerge victorious from one of the most critical episodes of his life. In the space of a few minutes he entered the world of microbes, adapted to the atmosphere, separated from the placenta, started to use his lungs and breathe independently, and adapted to the force of gravity and differences in temperature. Jesus is a hero!

There was no clock in the stable. Mary did not try to time how long Jesus was at the breast before he fell asleep. During the first night after birth Mary had only a few bouts of light sleep; she was vigilant and protective, and anxious to meet the needs of the most precious little creature on earth.

In the days that followed, Mary learned to recognise when her baby wanted to be rocked. She was so in tune with him that she could perfectly adapt the rhythm of the rocking movements to the demands of the baby. While rocking, Mary started to croon tunes, and words were added. Like millions of other mothers she had discovered lullabies. This is how Jesus started to learn about movement and, therefore, about space. This is how he started to learn about rhythm and, therefore, about time. He was gradually entering a space and time reality. As baby Jesus grew, Mary began to introduce more and more words into her lullabies and this is how Jesus learned his mother tongue.

Reference

1 Lorber, J. *Die Jugend Jesu.* Stuttgart, Lorber Verlag, Bietigheim/ Wurtemberg, 1852.

20   *Homo Ecologicus*

Questions Special to our Time

The scientification of Love is occurring at the very time when the dramatic increase in destructive behaviour, including self-destructive behaviour, inspires a great number of questions and much research. Suicides, drug addictions, murders and other forms of violence are major causes of deaths and handicaps among those born during the last decades of the twentieth century.

The scientification of love coincides also with a sudden and shocking new awareness of the Earth's vulnerability. Ecological awareness has come about cumulatively as a result of a great number and variety of symptoms of 'planetary overload'. These are well known. No one is unaware of the altered composition of the atmosphere, the accumulation of 'greenhouse gases' and ozone depletion in the stratosphere. We all know that the planetary resources are rapidly being depleted – fossil fuels are being depleted, agricultural lands becoming deserts; there is a shortage of water and a depletion of what we had thought of as inexhaustible fish stocks. Animal, marine, bird and plant species are becoming extinct and there is widespread pollution of the sea food chain and the land food chain from man-made toxic chemicals. Ill health in cattle is an effect of industrialised farming. There are unexplored territories. It is not yet well understood that the most serious aspect of pollution is intrauterine pollution. The human body accumulates, over the years, synthetic chemicals that would not have been there 50 years ago. They are transmitted to the foetus via the placenta at critical phases of its development. The spectacular fall of the average sperm count since the middle of the twentieth century is currently interpreted as one of the most visible long-term effects of intrauterine pollution.

It is quite usual to claim that the solution to our ecological crises will require changes in social and political structures, in technology, in scientific research, in economic activities, in our values and in our philosophical systems. It has not yet been recognised that the solution to the conflict between mankind and planet Earth depends, first and foremost, on the way *Homo* evolves.[1] We need a sort of non-genetic mutation initiated by necessity, reason and scientific knowledge if the planet is to sustain human life in the future.

If the planet remains inhabitable – a hypothesis I refuse to discount – it implies that *'Homo Superpredator'* will eventually be overtaken by *'Homo Ecologicus'*. *Homo Ecologicus* will be characterised by a propensity to unite and establish a global awareness, and also by an ability to develop a fundamental respect for Mother Earth.

Finally, the most urgent problems humankind has to face are all related to different aspects of the capacity to love, including a compassionate interest in unborn generations. That is why the scientification of love must be recognised as a vital aspect of the scientific revolution. A conjunction of scientific data indicates that the period surrounding birth appears as the critical link in the chain of events on which it is possible to effectively act.

Such considerations cannot be dissociated from the context of the twenty-first century. Where the birth of humans is concerned, we are in an unprecedented situation. Although all known societies always had a tendency to interfere in the birth process, until recently a woman could not have a baby without releasing a complex cocktail of 'hormones of love'. Today, for the first time in the history of humankind, most women, in many countries, become mothers without having their brain impregnated with such hormones. They can rely on pharmacological hormonal substitutes that are not 'love hormones'. For example an epidural anaesthesia can replace the release of endorphins, and a drip of synthetic oxytocin can replace the natural hormone. Furthermore a great proportion of babies are born by caesarean section. The questions must be raised in terms of civilisation. Can humanity survive obstetrics?

Obstacles

The priority is to radically and urgently reconsider how babies are born in order to disturb as little as possible the interaction between the mothers and their newborn infants.

The most important obstacle is a deep-rooted cultural misunderstanding of birth physiology. This misunderstanding is easy to explain. For thousands of years all human groups have established and transmitted from generation to generation subtle ways to interfere in the physiological processes. This was related to the evolutionary advantage of developing the human potential for aggressiveness and of controlling the development of the capacity to love.

This misunderstanding was not radically modified when different schools of 'natural childbirth' emerged in the middle of the twentieth century. Although the terms 'method' and 'natural' are difficult to reconcile, the most influential 'natural childbirth movement' was the 'psychoprophylactic method' or 'Lamaze method', based on the concept of 'conditioned reflexes' introduced in Russia by Pavlov and his disciples. The team of Russian researchers had understood that during the birth process the inhibitions originate in the neocortex, the part of the brain that is highly developed among humans; however, they ignored the idea that a reduction of control by the neocortex is the most important aspect of birth physiology. Instead of coming to the conclusion that a labouring woman needs first to be protected against any sort of neocortical stimulation, they based their strategy on reconditioning mothers-to-be. Women were conditioned to control the way they were breathing and the noise they were making. An active role was given to educators and birth attendants, and, incidentally, to the neocortex of labouring women. The Lamaze method's interventionist philosophy fitted well with American medicine's own interventionism.[2] It reinforced the vision of the birth process as a voluntary process. Lamaze's teaching was acceptable at a time when the midwife as a mother figure had disappeared. The birth attendant became an active 'coach'.

The point of view of Grantly Dick-Read, in the UK, was based on the clinical observations of an experienced practitioner. Read did not refer to the neocortex, but he gave a perfect description, with the language he could use in the 1930s and 1940s, of the effects of the physiological reduction of the neocortical control during labour. He wrote, for example, that the secret for rapid cervical dilatation is 'disassociation of the mind from the mechanism of the uterus', and that 'any effort to assist actively or to reinforce normal first stage contractions is designed to defeat its own end'.[3] About the second stage, he described the mother-to-be as 'oblivious to her surroundings, and careless of her appearance, expression and speech'. Because Read has never rethought the postures imposed by a table or a bed, he was not aware of the most unexpected positions in which the mother-to-be might find herself. For this excellent observer it was obvious that fear is the most common cause of difficult and painful labour. According to his theory, fear creates muscular tension that gives rise to pain in labour. In the scientific context of the first half of the twentieth century, he could not interpret the cause-and-effect relationship between fear, muscular tension and difficult birth. He could not explain the association of fear and release of adrenaline. He could not know that adrenaline inhibits the birth process by interfering with the release and the action of oxytocin. At that time nobody could explain clearly that the increased muscular tone induced by fear is an associated effect of the release of adrenaline. Dick-Read claimed that childbirth should not be painful because there are no examples of painful physiological processes. Today, since the discovery of the system of 'endorphins', one can accept that there is a physiological pain during labour and also a physiological system of protection against pain. Dick-Read's point of view led to a method of childbirth preparation. It consists of educating women about the anatomy and physiology of labour and of training them in progressive relaxation techniques. In spite of his perfect understanding of fear as the main cause of difficult birth, Dick-Read did not seem to be interested in the nature of midwifery. He did not refer to the authentic midwife as a mother figure with whom labouring women can get rid of their fear and feel secure. At the time when pioneers such as Lamaze and Dick-Read were practising and theorising, there were no easy scientific answers to complex puzzles.

To the deep-rooted cultural misunderstanding of birth physiology we must add other obstacles, particularly the current lack of motivation for studying the environmental factors that influence the birth process. This lack of motivation is understandable.

We are entering the age of elective 'caesarean section on request'. This new phenomenon developed originally in Italy[4] and in the largest Latin American cities. Today it is found all over the world. Certain obstetricians are indirectly participating in its rapid development. For example 31 per cent of London female obstetricians with an uncomplicated pregnancy at term claimed that they would choose an elective caesarean delivery for themselves.[5] Similar preferences have been expressed among female and male North American obstetricians.[6]

Philip Steer, a Professor of Obstetrics in London, underlined that the human brain size represents the main challenge to the birth process. He considers caesarean section an 'evolving procedure', that is a technological solution to 'the conflict between the need to think and the need to run'.[7] He anticipates that the procedure will become so safe that for most women the unpredictable risks of labour will no longer be justified. If caesarean section becomes the norm average birth weight will no longer be restricted by the constraints of maternal pelvic size, so that eventually caesarean birth becomes necessary for the majority. I heard another Professor of Obstetrics who was wondering why there are still women who want to go through the pain and stress of labour while it is possible, with a drip and epidural, to give birth vaginally and watch the TV at the same time.

It is obvious that many childbirth experts find it difficult to see beyond the period surrounding birth and to think in terms of civilisation. They have lost the intuitive knowledge many women (and some men) still have.

Reasons for hope and optimism

In spite of these apparently insurmountable obstacles there are reasons for hope and optimism. Scientific knowledge can induce awareness. The advent of *Homo Ecologicus* is not utopian. In the age of the Scientification of Love humanity has the keys to invent new strategies for survival.

Summary

Reasons for anxiety. Today, for the first time in the history of humankind, most women, in many countries, become mothers without releasing a complex cocktail of hormones of love. The questions must be raised in terms of civilisation. Can Humanity survive obstetrics?

Reasons for hope and optimism. In the age of the Scientification of Love, Humanity has the keys to invent new strategies for survival. The advent of *Homo Ecologicus* is not utopian.

References

1 Odent, M. *Genèse de l'homme écologique.* Epi, Paris, 1979.
2 Lamaze, F. *Painless childbirth.* Pocket Books, New York, 1965.
3 Dick-Read, G. *Childbirth without fear.* Harper and Brothers, London, 1944.
4 Tranquilli, A.L. and Garzetti, G.G. 'A new ethical and clinical dilemma in obstetric practice: caesarean section on "maternal request".' *Am. J. Obstet. Gynecol.* 1997; 177: 245–6.
5 Al-Mufti, R., McCarthy, A. and Fisk, N.M. 'Survey of obstetricians' personal preference and discretionary practice.' *Eur. J. Obstet. Gynecol. Reprod. Biol.* 1997; 73: 1–4.
6 Gabbe, S.G. and Holzman, G.B. 'Obstetricians' choice of delivery.' *Lancet* 2001; 357: 722.
7 Steer, P. 'Caesarean section: an evolving procedure?' *Brit. J. Obstet. Gynecol.* 1998; 105: 1052–5.

Index